Effortless Learning:

Learn The Secrets That Teachers Never Told You: Master Any Subject, Memorize More, And Focus Fast

(WHILE STUDYING LESS)

Tony Roe

Table Of Contents

CHAPTER 1

A Little Story....

I would like to first congratulate you for purchasing this book. The fact that you are buying this book indicates your seriousness about getting the best of learning, no matter how good or poor your grades are right now. You are determined to improve it, aren't you!

Whether you are a consistent student or someone that wants to accelerate their learning, this book will help you improve your grades in ways that are both smart and fun.

One of the reasons I have written this book is because I used to be very playful, mischievous and sometimes even plain lazy and didn't care much about studies. But after I learnt the right techniques and strategies for studying, my results improved tremendously in comparison with our peers. We were even asked to teach our peers the methods of studying.

The techniques and strategies that are going to be shared with you in this book are some of the most useful methods that have ever been taught so far. Many students have been benefited and have shown tremendous improvement in their study skills. And many have become good professionals in the field of medicine, engineering and law although they scored poorly in exams during school days. Sounds interesting, doesn't it!

Ohhhh! By the way, are you getting a lot of the F's now? Well, just follow the guidelines we suggest and see how your grades shoot up.

Turning my life around from failures to A's...

I was an average kid when young. I neither scored very bad in my exams nor did I score very well to top the class. At the age of 12, I was considered a good boy with normal grades and that helped me go to a good school.

When I was 13 and in my new school, I bought a play station without my parent's knowledge and I started playing lots of games everyday. Besides play station, I also played a card game know as "magic" cards. I wasted lot of money while playing this game. I got so addicted to these games that sometimes I even went to the extent of stealing money from my parents' wallets. Eventually my grades started plunging and I had a hard time coping with my homework.

In the group of new friends, I found myself playing the games almost everyday. While playing these games we came across another interesting game called 'counter strike and half life'. We spent most of our days and most of the nights until 11p.m playing these games.

My parents, especially my mother was very worried about my grades and as a result, my parent's hired tuition teachers for me. By the time I progressed to secondary 4, I had 2 tuition teachers, one teaching me physics and mathematics and the other English. But, I still failed during my mid year exams.

I didn't play as many games as before because I was really scared that I would not do well in Cambridge 'O' level exams. Luckily, by the end of all these tuitions, my results were not that bad and I managed to get into a neighborhood junior college.

Before the 'O' level results are released, students enter college with their preliminary results obtained from their school. So my preliminary results actually brought me to the 5th junior college in Singapore because the results were moderated by 4 points.

But when the 'O' level results were out, I was kicked out by the college because my results weren't as good as others. So my only choice was to enter a neighborhood college. My parents and I actually pleaded with the principal to let me stay in the college, but the principal only accepted in such cases, students with special talents or those who were rich enough to donate money to the school.

The World is rather cruel...

This was the most memorable incident of my life and it gave me a powerful desire and a very strong motivation to excel in my grades and prove to that principal what a mistake he had made in deciding not to allow me to study in that college.

For the first year of my college life, I actually failed quite a number of times. Due to my consistent and persistent effort put into studies, my results improved but at a very slow rate.

It was then that I learnt some skills that changed my grades.

It was at the end of the first year in college, I came upon a few books that showed me the strategies and techniques to acquire excellent grades.

The books taught me numerous techniques which accelerated my learning curve. I learnt that the reason I got my poor results was not because I was stupid, slow, or the exams were difficult, but because I didn't know the appropriate techniques for studying. I didn't pay attention to classes, didn't do my homework and didn't practice enough.

Having learnt a few new techniques, I got so excited that I applied them to my studying immediately and continued even during the holidays when everyone was playing. Many friends thought I was crazy to study when it was time to relax. Some even told me to stop pretending to be a hard worker. However, no amounts of criticisms or comments stopped me.

I even told everyone that I'm going to get triple A's for my preliminary exams and 'A' level. However, everyone treated me like an idiot, commenting that getting distinctions for my 3 core subjects was impossible given the type of person they thought I were.

Besides, for a student to get 3 distinctions in a neighborhood college, it was mission impossible. But I didn't care about what they said and began to take elaborate actions, consistent effort, and built a lot of momentum in my studies. "I WILL PROVE THEM WRONG!" was what kept me going.

Together with the right strategies and the strong desire to excel, my results started to show great improvement. The grades were improving at the rate of a grade, every time there was a test or exam. At the end of my first year, I got the grades BCD. In the next test I had ABC, followed by AAB and then finally during 'A' level, I did get AAA.

I'm telling you my story not to boast about myself but to dawn upon you that to achieve excellent grades, it does not matter whether you are intelligent, clever, or smart, but what matters is the desire to do well and have the right techniques and strategies to study in a smart way.

I'm going to show you exactly how I produced my results, and guide you so that you can have the same results as me, and/or maybe do better than I actually did.

What can you expect from this book?

If you are looking for something that is going to help you score well in your exams, or accelerate your learning overnight then I'm sorry I can't help you. After all these years of failures in studies, I learnt one important lesson. You can't just get A's by studying the day before the exams. You can't get A's if you don't practice at all. And you can't pass if you don't study at all.

This book can only help you if you want to succeed in your studies. To succeed you must be willing to put in the best of your efforts and you must not be satisfied with mere pass marks.

One of the reasons I did well for my 'A' level is also because I realized the importance of studying. I realized how important it was to get a distinction so no one would ever look down upon me in terms of studies and no one can ever disqualify me for something because I didn't have a good grade.

After all, getting a very good grade is about finding a better career that you can choose instead of people choosing you. And due to the fast growing competitive society, obtaining a good grade is a must for you to choose your first career.

So what are we waiting for......Let's get started...

Why Are You Not REALLY The One That Is At Fault For NOT Scoring A's In Exams?

What!!!!!! I am not at FAULT?

Yes. You are reading this right. I know that you don't read such a statement so often.

And No, I am not sugarcoating you so that you will like me and give me a resounding testimonial for this e-book.

Scoring As' really centers around 2 THINGS and they are your **LEARNING strategies** and EXAM/APPLICATION strategies.

Let me be brutally honest with you. The education system in schools does not teach you these effective learning strategies that will help you get As' every time.

Isn't it an obnoxious bold claim by me? Far from it

Let me give you some examples of poor learning strategies that you think are effective. Note-taking instead of note-making, making linear notes instead of whole brain notes, and reading slowly versus power reading; are some of the poor strategies and the list goes on and on. (Later chapters reveal many such poor strategies)

But first, let's take a quick look into the meaning of learning.

Learning is simply gaining knowledge and skills through study or experience while education is testing your results of such learning through exams.

However, we often miss out an important step and that is the actual process of learning.

What happens very often in schools is that teachers focus too much on transferring loads of information into students because the syllabus recommends that the given workload is completed within that time frame. Sounds familiar, doesn't it. Of course it does.

A teacher unloads his 'truckload' of information which sometimes drowns the students. Most often students sit helplessly at the edge, hanging on to keep up with the pace and the information.

This model of education could still work if the teachers have guided their students to the process of learning before they deliver the main contents.

For example, what specific action should a student take before going for the class that will help improve his understanding greatly? Are there any particular reading strategies to increase comprehension?

In fact, it is this 'process of learning' that is so powerful and is the fact that many see it as the 'Secrets of Scoring As'.

So Why Are The Schools Not Teaching The 'Secrets of Scoring As' !

Take a look around you. Are there students scoring straight As' with little or no effort? They most probably have an older copy of 'Secrets of Scoring As'.

What! How did they secure such a copy?

No... They did not buy a copy from me. How did they uncover the secretive 'process of learning' then? Honestly, there are a few ways to do so.

1. He learnt the 'process of learning' from a senior.

This strategy works great. Seniors have been there and done that. They are qualified to guide you to avoid certain pitfalls. However not many seniors are consistent 'A' students as well. Some would probably be good tutors but they themselves are unclear of the secretive 'process of learning'.

2. Massive amount of trial and error.

This is a group of students that is worth attention. Out of a group of 10, perhaps only 1 will uncover the 'Secrets of scoring As', the rest will continue to bury their heads in the books to get those As'. To be that unique individual of uncovering the 'Secrets of Scoring As', it will take great efforts of trial and error to find out what works and what does not. If you are willing to grit your teeth and keep applying study and exam strategies over and over again, you will progress from studying hard to studying smart.

3. You read up heavily in the area of accelerated learning.

Now, this can be a chore for some of you. Playing is fine, in fact it is excellent but when it comes to reading outside curriculum, are fashion magazines you're only reading diet! But there will always be a handful of students who are EAGER to do well in exams. All it takes is the common sense to find books on Accelerated Learning and start extracting and applying the concepts. That's the hard part. Most books are not written for the purpose of scoring As', which means you have to adopt, adapt and apply until it works. It can be extremely time-consuming.

Last but not the least; schools are in fact bringing some concepts mentioned in this book to your curriculum albeit at a much slower and superficial level at the moment. Honestly, if everyone knows about these powerful learning strategies in this book, the education system will have to re-invent itself. It won't be the scenario of 'F' student and 'A' student, but would most probably be a battle of 'A' students and even more 'A' students. Nevertheless, this will eventually happen. Hence it's important that you are ahead of the crowd, and be the one riding the waves as early as possible.

Next, you will learn how this set of 'learning strategies' found in this book will empower you to study SMART and score 'A' more consistently.

The Traditional Learning Path

"Do not go where the path may lead, go instead where there is no path and leave a trail." Ralph Waldo Emerson

To learn anything successfully, you have to go through 4 phases of learning. This is the traditional path of learning.

Phase 1 - We don't know what we don't know

"Ignorance is bliss." You don't know and you are unaware that you don't know. A good example would be the best subject you are doing well in school now. Once upon a time, you did not know anything about it, you were not even aware of its existence. Now, you are starting to be aware of that.

Phase 2 - We know what we don't know

This is the start of your learning journey. You are not very good with the subject yet. But you are learning rapidly. You have an idea of what you don't know. By filling the gap, you get immediate results.

Phase 3 - Can do if I know how to

You have a good grasp of the basic understandings of the subject. Simple questions regarding the subject can be solved with some effort and concentration. You can do if you know how to. Improvements take a longer time to happen. You stumble when faced with more difficult questions.

Phase 4 - Can do all with effort

This is the final stage of your learning. All 'A' students strive for this mastery. No question really terrifies you anymore. With effort, concentration and some thinking, the toughest nut can be cracked by you.

Congratulations! You have achieved an 'A' student status!

It takes roughly 1000 hours to bring a subject to Phase 3. Some of you may be gasping now, but this is the ground reality. Do a simple math calculation to verify. The most- likely action a student would take is to give up. Hardworking ones will bury their head and grit their teeth to make the 'A' grades happen.

How to Jump from Phase 2 to 4 in the Shortest Time Possible?

The answer is ALWAYS in the pudding, so-to-speak. And the pudding is the book you are reading now. In fact, the strategies outlined are so practical that it feels like we are teaching you to 'cheat' the traditional learning path.

All the risk is reversed on us however. We have suffered the 'F' grades. Tired and fed up, we went in search of the solutions and got an overload of information. Some were useful, but some a complete waste of time. Tested, tested once more and re-tested again. All the research is here now, with trial and error done for you.

The only missing ingredient is having you to consider and apply each strategy outlined in this book CONSISTENTLY! And you will like the outcome at the end of the year. How much you will grow mentally during the process will surely be amazing.

Hence, the one thing I need you to really do now is to empty out all the strategies you have been using for learning. Chuck it aside. Have an open mind and start receiving new inputs that will change the way you study for the better!

CHAPTER 2
The Secrets of Learning

How do normal people learn?

Have you ever wondered how we learn? This is typically how an average student will learn. The boxes represent the lessons you attend in the school. The average students who put in effort by paying attention to classes and doing homework will at least reach level (4) of the learning experience when they have a test.

For the more playful students who skip lessons, do not pay attention to the classes and never do their homework, they would learn nothing and would be at level (0) of their learning curve when they take the test.

Can you see guess how much they would score in their exams? The student at level 0 would score pathetic and the other one who is at level (4) would score higher. So how do you actually score A's when others only score B, C or D's? The only way you can outplay them is by gaining more learning experience of the subject you are studying.

Here's an **example of a better student**.

Before each lesson, the 'clever' students would read through the notes and do their best to understand it before attending the lessons. As they attend the class, they would be able to understand better, and clarify points with the teacher what they do not really understand.

As the lesson gets complete for the day, they would revise what they had learnt that day. The average student who didn't revise would be one step behind these 'clever' students.

The next day, they would start doing their homework. The 'clever' students, upon reaching home, would attempt recalling all the lessons taught from the first day onwards. It may be just a short learning time. This way they would be 2-3 steps ahead of the average student.

After the assignment and before the test, they would practice more exam questions, and master most of the questions. The average student never practices the questions.

Look where the better students are now? They are 3-4 steps ahead of the average students. Don't you think these students would score better? Certainly.

During the test, while others are at level (4), a clever student is at level (8) of his learning curve. He therefore has a high percentage of scoring better than the other students.

As you can see, the more you revise, the better you are at that particular topic. Some people go even more than level (8) or (9) to make sure they can score at least an A's. The actual fact is that they don't need to spend much time on (1), (3), (5). These little activities only take a short while to do if you follow the strategies in the book systematically.

However, if you didn't revise or relearn the topic after a period of time, your level of experience with the topics would decrease. And you may need more effort to gain back that experience than if you would have consistently done your revision.

This is how the top A's student differs from the average student.

The way to beat anyone in studies and learning is by increasing your learning experiences. The more learning experience you have in the subjects, the easier for you to be the top.

Getting As' For Subjects You Hate

Most of the time, students have no problem getting As' for the topics they love. Some can even sit for the test without studying but still score distinctions. These are the subjects that most students would pay the most attention to. And whenever they have homework, they would finish their favorite subjects first.

The real challenge is scoring As' for the subjects you hate.

"Argh... I don't want to score A's for that!," Some students told that to me.

I'm not going to force you to do something that you don't want to. I'm only going to share this with you if you are willing to do it. It is for you to DECIDE that you will no longer tolerate having bad results and that you will do whatever it takes to get A's.

Here's the answer. If you are weak at a particular subject, it means that you will have to do more of it. There's no way to escape. If you look at the previous learning experience, to master a subject and to score well for the subject, you would need to gain the learning level of your learning curve. The more you practice, the better you get.

In my high school days, I used to hate Physics because I found it a difficult subject with hard-to-grasp concepts. It was only when I reached my college days that I decided that I MUST get an A for my physics. And that was when I really experienced many painful months to build the foundations in physics. It was not easy as my foundation was weak and college physics is rather difficult. But I had to do it.

So I started to practice by spending more time and effort asking questions, understanding and memorizing the concepts, revising what I had been taught. Gradually, my physics started to improve.

And in the end, I got my A. Now, I no longer hate physics.

This applies to you as well, do more of what you hate and you will get better.

Do you feel MESSED UP sometimes?

Have you attended a class that you feel confused when you have actually finished the lessons? Do you feel sometimes that you don't understand what the teachers are talking about? Do you get worried that you may fail the exams? Do you feel that it's a total mess? I sometimes do, and I'm sure you do too.

Most students get frustrated when they are confused and especially when they don't understand what the teacher is teaching. And they would just shut their mind off from thinking and avoid the topics as much as they can.

What is confused anyway?

I believe that confused is a process whereby your brain is figuring out something new you have learnt. When you get confused, your brain is actually learning something new that is not easy to comprehend. When you make effort to understand, the process actually helps you to become more intelligent and clever. And when you finally understand what you have learnt, you will go, "Aaah..... I finally get it!"

When the students avoid the topics and questions that are confusing to them, they stop thinking and learning something new. As times goes by, they won't be able to answer any questions in exams because they can't cope with the learning demands. They won't be able to answer the exams in the future. And the next thing they know is POOR GRADES.

Top students when encountered with the confusing problems, will actually embrace it. They will look at similar problems to find a solution. They will rack their brain before they finally ask their friends or teachers for help.

The truth in getting confused is beneficial because it only means you are going to learn something new, hence your intelligent level is increasing, and you are getting smarter. What would you learn if you don't get confused? You will learn something but nothing as significant.

The Fastest Way To Learn Something New

Interested in learning as fast as the speeding bullet?

If you ever want to learn something very fast, the best way is to MAKE A LOT OF MISTAKES. What you can do is take the exam papers to practice as many questions as possible. Even if you feel that the questions are difficult, you do your best to think through the questions and attempt the questions.

You will find out that you make plenty of mistakes, even as much as 80%-90%. It's alright. But after you made the mistakes, go through your mistakes and find the right answers and steps for the questions. Ask someone who knows how to answer such questions to help you.

You would require going through the thinking process, doing your best to do even when you don't know. You may make a lot of mistakes; get very frustrated and feel like giving up, but continue to force yourself. The best choice is to refer to your notes to help you. And after reading the answers, you would require to understand the solutions and do the question again by yourself.

This may be a very painful process, but you are going to learn very fast once you catch up with the technique.

My advice to those who are going to use this method is to only use this method when you are VERY DETERMINED to score As' or be the top student.

It is not a very easy learning process. You may get so frustrated sometimes that you don't feel like learning anymore. So it is recommended only to those who are very serious in getting As'.

But this proves the previous points as well that if you can pick things up very fast although you feel it's confusing, you can still endure the process of learning.

The Difference between the Best and the Worst

When I was rejected by the college principal due to my poor results, I felt like a failure. I could not understand why I had to study so hard for my 'O' level and still get such poor grades. I could not understand why some of my friends who didn't study so hard during the past year and some of the students who scored poor the past year could become suddenly so good in the next year.

It took me a while to realize these facts, to realize the difference between the successful people and the average people.

It is in the ACTION

Everyone thinks that the successful people are smart, clever and capable of great achievements. But they don't notice that the difference between the successful people and the average people is the ACTION they take. Successful people don't turn successful overnight. Successful people become successful because they took solid ACTION. And different actions create different results.

If you look into the context of study, we are caught in the trap of seeing how excellent the top students scored in their exams and think they get all distinctions because they are clever, smart, intelligent, or have some special talent.

But the truth between the performance of top students and the average students is their ability to get them selves to take action. And that's what each one of us can do. After all, everyone has the capacity the top students have.

But it is the top students that know what actions would produce what kind of results, and be able to take the kind of actions that produce the results they want.

That's simply the truth.

If you want to produce the same results as the top students, it's just as simple as to model the kind of actions they took and you will produce the same results (it maybe better or not as good depending on how you do it).

I have seen students who have poor results in their high school but turn out to be a scholar in the university after taking the right actions.

What actions produce what kind of results?

Just like Newton's third law of motion, (for every action, there is an equal and opposite reaction), how you study determines your grades.

Back in my college days, I had a few friends that stuck together during classes and breaks. All of us came from different schools with different results. You can say that not all of us were clever, smart or intelligent.

So during breaks and those free periods, we were together as a team working on our studies, while the other classmates spend their time on other things like playing, chatting, or copying homework.

My group of friends often did the same thing and at the end, almost all our results were the same. While my other classmates who spend their time on other things got different results.

From this, you can categorize the students into different groups depending on how they study. I did actually ask them how they usually studied.

Failures....uffff - These students often study during the last minute and hence have no time to cover everything. And they usually only have the time to read through the textbooks and pray they can pass. Some of them don't listen in class and often skip them.

The Cs' or the Ds' students - They manage to memorize some of the notes, understand the important points and then jump into the exams.

Bs' maybe sometimes As' - These are the students that listen in the class, memorize their notes, practice some of the questions and then go for the exams.

So what do the As' students always do?

A brief outline on what the As' students do is

1. Understand what is being taught

2. Memorize all the topics coming up for exams

3. Practice different types of question that may appear in exams

4. Perform the above 3 steps a number of times

The whole book will give you the strategies they used to consistently produce A's. But for now, I'm going to share with you the most important formula to score A's.

As I have said, the results you get are determined by the actions you take. RESULTS

ACTIONS

So what determines the Actions you take? What causes some to work so hard while the others to slack like nobody's business? And what causes the top student to know how to study effectively while the average students don't know?

It is the attitude and the knowledge that makes you take different actions from your friends. Attitudes are the mindset and beliefs of what you think of life. With different attitudes, you would take different actions.

The Success Mindset

Do you want to succeed?

"Yes. Of course I want to succeed. What a stupid question to ask."

Isn't that what everyone would say if I ask them this question? So if everyone wants to succeed, why isn't everyone succeeding and living comfortably?

The reason why some people succeed while the most don't is because large percentages of the people don't make the decision to succeed. They don't make the commitment to succeed.

They may want to succeed but deep down inside, they don't have the desire to succeed, and when they encounter any difficulty, they would just give up.

Do you think that successful people are always successful? No. They don't always get successful. In fact, they have been through many failures but they never give up. The great difference between successful people and average people is because the successful people MAKE a DECISION to succeed. And they DO WHATEVER IT TAKES to achieve their goals.

Students who score As' in their exams are the same as well. After they make a decision to score As', they will do whatever it takes to score As'. They will not accept anything less. They will study for 10-16 hours a day, staying up even when they are very tired. They will ask the teachers questions until they are satisfied with the answers.

They may not get A's for some of the time, but they will say "_Hey, I'm going to learn from my mistakes and continue to do my best for the following test_." And when they see a question they don't have any idea how to do, they would rake their brain and look into the books to find the methods and solutions.

Before the teachers tell them to finish their tutorials or assignments, they are ready to hand in and they are on the way finishing the others.

Whenever they are asked to hang out with friends, they would say "no".

It's only when they finish revising, doing all the homework, the projects and studying for tests that they allow themselves to enjoy for a while.

Chances are high that they will eventually succeed and score As' if they consistently put in the effort and taking solid ACTION.

But if you look at the average students, they say they want to score well for their exams, but still they end up watching television and playing computer games. They wait till the last minute to revise for their tests or finishing up their homework.

They don't do enough for whatever it takes to score an A. If they get an A, they will be happy about it, if not it's ok. Some even say "what's the use of studying so well".
That is why they won't score As'.

There are 3 types of people in the world. These 3 types of people produce different type of results.

The first type of students is the ones who the teachers don't really like because they usually do less than expected. When the teachers give them assignments to do, they usually don't finish them, or never do at all, or even copy in school. These are the students that usually score badly for exams because they do LESS THAN EXPECTED. Around 50% of the students fall into this category.

There is this second type of students that always finish what the teachers ask them to do. Nothing more, nothing less. They only do what they are expected to do. These are the students who are able to pass the exams, but not really scoring with high marks. Around 45% of the students fall into such category.

And for this third category of students, they always do more than expected. When the teachers actually tell them to do a piece of composition, they would actually do more than what the teachers expect them to do. Besides doing the homework the teachers give, they will continue with additional assignments. These are the students that are at the top 5% of the school.

Which category do you fall into? It's up to you to decide.

ULTIMATE SUCCESS FORMULA

Anthony Robbins talks about this formula that every successful student uses.

It always starts with GOALS. The successful students always know their outcome, what results they want, what are they going to do in the future, their future career, etc.

Only when you know what your goals are, can you plan about how you are going to get there and take the necessary ACTIONS towards your goals. You will find the necessary STRATEGIES to reach that goal.

When you take action, you will produce 2 kinds of results, one is success, and the other is failure.

A successful student when encounters failure, will change his strategies, learning from his mistakes and continue to take massive action. As long as he continues to change his strategies, continues to put in the effort, he will eventually succeed in his studies.

An average student would just give up when he meets failure.

So let me start by asking you one of the most important questions.

What do you want in life?

If I told you this, I don't think you would believe me. But this is the most important lesson I have learnt in life. This is the reason that helped many people including me become successful (for me success was getting As'). This is the one reason that differentiates the As' from the Bs'. Excellent compared to Decent.

I'm going to share with you the reasons I scored As'. The reason I scored As' is because I designed my destiny. I got 3 distinctions in my 'A' Level not because I was lucky, smart or knew all the strategies to study smart, but it's because I created this design for destiny.

To tell you the truth, before the end of my first year in college, I actually sat and wrote down what I wanted in life. What were my dreams, my hopes, desires and how would I want my future life to be shaped. I spent a few days designing and writing down what kind of life I wanted to have 5 years, 10 years, 20 years down the road. I also wrote down what were the things I wouldn't want. I wrote down that I wanted to score 3 As' for my 'A' level and to enter the local university of business. I wrote down I wanted to pass my driving test in the first attempt.

And right now the first few have come true. Now, I'm making my way to bigger goals and bigger dreams.

What I want to say is, I am where I am right now because I had a dream, the dream that I wanted to create. It all begins with a dream.

That's how all cities are being built, schools being set up, and heroes are coming up. It all began with a dream, a desire, a GOAL.

IF ACHIEVING OR SUCCESS IS SO EASY, WHY ISN'T EVERYONE SUCCESSFUL?

Many people always say that if it's so easy to be successful, everyone would be successful. Does that happen just by setting a goal?

The difference between successful people and average people is to take ACTION and to bring their goals into reality.

How do we set goals?

The goal must be Specific.

Why do you need to be specific? If I were to ask you to find a person called Benjamin, would you be able to find him?

Could be "Yes", but he may not be the person I want.

What if I ask you to find a person called Benjamin Chan R.T.? Would you be able to find him? No, you may not know where to find him and don't know who is he.

But what if I told you to look for him in a building XXX at the 5th floor, would you be able to find him? Yes, most likely.

The same applies to goal setting. You need to be as specific as possible. Don't just say you want to score well for your exams. Write down what grades you want to have, for which subjects, how many marks.

I wrote down I want to score As' for my 3 subjects, Math, Physics and Chemistry at 'A' Level standard.

Mathematics – 85 marks
Physics – 80 marks
Chemistry – 80 marks

These marks are what I wanted to get in my preliminary results. And I actually got 75 in physics, around 75 in chemistry and 82 in math.

Look how powerful it is to be as specific as you can. Write down your goals now. **Be as specific as possible.**

Motivating

Your goal must be to be always motivated. So to keep your motivation going strong and consistent, you must have a BIG Goal. It's not just a small little B, but As'. Everyday when I wake up, I feel motivated because I feel that I'm working towards my goal. When there is no motivation, reaching the goal is not going to be easy.

Next, why do you want that goal? What do you achieve from it? What are the reasons that would make you strive achieve your goals even if you already failed many times and felt like giving up? Write down all the benefits you will get from achieving your goals. STOP and WRITE it all down NOW.

Measurable

To reach your goals, you need a plan to check whether you are on the right path of achievement. To do that, you will need to measure your progress.

The way I measured my progress was by evaluating my performance in all the small tests that the teachers gave. I knew that in order to get 3 A's, I would require to know my topics very well. This thought applies to you as well.

You will need to know that you are scoring A or at least B in the tests to know that you are on the right track. If you didn't score well for any of the test, it's time to look at where you have gone wrong in your study pattern and correct it. From the test, you would also know which topics you require to put in more effort.

Plan

You would also need to work out a plan to reach your goals. If you don't have a plan, you will not know what to do each day. For instance, you can plan that before the start of each lesson you will read through the book and do your best to understand. Then after the teacher has taught that lesson, you will dedicate some time every day (2 hours for example) to memorize or revise the things you have learnt.

Deadline

You need to give yourself a time limit to the deadline. Make sure you give yourself a deadline to reach your deadline. The deadline can't be too short nor should it take forever to reach your goal.

Set a realistic and achievable deadline to reach your goal.

Action

After writing your goals, it's time to take action, to start doing the small little things that keep you going to reach your goals.

You would need to gain the momentum to start because some people after making goals procrastinate and after a while, they simply stop working towards the goal.

Thus, it's essential to start doing activities in small steps [also referred to as baby steps] in your studies to keep you going.

Now it's time for you to write down your goals with the above guidelines. After that, we will go into the next topic.

CHAPTER 3
HOW TO STUDY SO MUCH IN SO LITTLE TIME

I am sure by now, you have a clear understanding between the differences of an average and an A student. It all boils down to learning strategies. We have exposed and explored the gap and now its time to close this gap.

ACCELERATED LEARNING STRATEGY #1 - POWER READING FOR INFORMATION

Reading your textbooks and course materials is an essential step when it comes to studying and preparing for exams. However, average students read the textbooks the wrong way, i.e. slowly and not extracting the essential information. And the worst part is that students are constantly referring to those textbooks at the eve of the exam for information. A mediocre strategy will result in mediocre results. Hence, this is where power reading comes into play.

'KEY' Information vs 'Not Useful' Information

'A' students recognize the vast difference between 'KEY' and 'Not Useful' information. In general, only 20% of the words found in your textbooks and course materials contain 'KEY' information. 'A' students focus their reading time on this 20% of the words and these words are known as KEYWORDS!

So, what are the 80% of the other words? They are words that contain no useful information. Connecting words like 'and', 'but', 'the', 'a' are non-keywords. Their only purpose is to link up the keywords together to allow you to have a better understanding when you are reading for the first time. However, they become an obstruction for the purpose of recalling and revision.

Hence, remember the 80/20 rule when reading your textbook and course materials.

Identifying and Harvesting THE <u>KEYWORDS</u>

So are you ready to tackle your textbooks and course materials for keywords? I hope you do.

The secret of power of reading to quickly read through your materials to extract the essence of the chapter you are studying by retrieving key ideas in the form of keywords.

Remember, keywords give you the gist/ key idea of the material you are studying. Connecting words add no value in helping you to recall and revise in the future.

What is Power Reading?

'A' students engage in power reading all the time. Power reading is speed reading your textbooks and course materials to extract key information. It is an effective strategy to handle written information. This strategy maximizes the use of time and effort and allows you to have a better level of comprehension. You will learn how to read faster and still maintain the same level of comprehension or even higher.

And all this can be achieved by learning how to extract key information.

The objective of Power Reading is to extract KEY information.

But most students are not aware of this strategy and they continue to plough through their course materials like 'an ox ploughing through the field'. Hence, the first learning strategy you have to start putting into practice would be 'POWER READING for Information!'

Why Power Read?

1. It is an Effective Strategy for Keywords Extraction
Power Reading the most effective strategy to extract key information in the form of keywords. These keywords could then be transferred into Mind Maps® which could be easily referred by you for the purpose of recalling and revision.

2. Increases Your Ability to Concentrate and Comprehend
Most students have the misconception that comprehension of a material comes only when you do it slowly. And that one can concentrate only if you take your time to read. The assumption sounds logical but the truth is reading fast will increase your ability to concentrate and comprehend. Research has shown that the faster you read, the better you comprehend.

What about concentration? It's the SAME! To have better concentration you need to occupy both sides of your brain. The inability to concentrate is because your brain (especially the creative right hemisphere of brain) is not occupied with any activity. This is what happens if you read too slowly. Your creative right brain wanders and thinks about other things.

3. Free Up More Time for Other 'Constructive Activities'
One of the facets of power reading is speed reading. Besides increasing your ability to concentrate and comprehend, it reduces the amount of time you spend reading as compared to your peers. An 'A' student will use the extra free time to read the material once more, thus increasing the level of comprehension. The free time can be used to relax, making notes or doing revision.

How Do Your Eyes Read?

Now, in this section you will learn how the eyes read. The movement of your eyes will determine your speed of reading. Hence, an understanding over this area will greatly aid you in mastering power reading.

So how do your eyes read?

Most people are not conscious about how their eyes read. While majority of you will conclude that your eyes move smoothly along the lines without pausing, the truth is that your eyes read by jumping from one point to another.

Usually each jump would cover more than one word, and pausing to absorb information. These pauses are important for the brain to absorb information. Each pause may last from 1/4 second to 1 ½ seconds. A good power reader will spend as little as 1/4 second or even lesser for each pause.

Hence, the first key to power reading is to cut down the time spent for each pause you take thus reducing the number of pauses our eyes make as they read.

Power Read More Than Once for Maximum Comprehension using the Same Amount of Time Your Peers Use!

Theory behind Power Reading

The question you should have in mind now is, "Why do I have to read more than once?" Simple, let me explain by giving you an analogy.

Student A watches a movie once.

Student B watches the same movie 7 times.

Who would have a better understanding, comprehension and better recall of the movie? Student B, of course!

This applies to power reading as well.

The next question that should be prodding you is 'How do I effectively power read more than once and have maximum comprehension rates?'

Step 1: Previewing

The brain seeks to see the wholeness in information. Hence before you read the text in depth, it is important for you to preview first. Previewing involves scanning and skimming the text to look for important information that you have to make note of.

When previewing, look for key ideas that are usually worded bold, italics or in the form of diagrams and pictures. And as you preview the text, you will have a clear picture of where the important ideas are, and this allows you to vary your reading speed as you proceed.

Reading the text in depth is like filling up the missing pieces to the almost complete jigsaw puzzle.

Step 2: Look for key ideas and keywords

The next step would be to go into the text in depth. Speed read the text with a pencil in hand and circle all the keywords presented. At the same time, for studying and examination purposes, start looking at the headlines and draft possible questions that might have the possibility of appearing in exams. This can be done more on an intuitive basis.

Step 3: Repeat the above step 3-5 times for maximum comprehension and effectiveness, taking lesser time with each round of power reading.

Step 4: Transfer all the keywords into a Mind Map (to be discussed in the next chapter)

Why Are You Not Reading Faster?

How fast you read depends on your reading habits! Unfortunately, the way we are taught reading when we are young, most people have developed a set of poor habits for reading. Here is a list of 'not very desirable' habits!

1. Lip-reading

Do you still remember how you were taught to read when you were young? The phonetics method was a common way to teach a child to read. In phonetics, 'the dog' is pronounced as 'dôg' and the child is asked to follow the pronunciation. Overtime, the child learns to pronounce the word but the habit of moving the lips while reading stays with him. Lip-reading slows down the speed with which a person is able to read. How fast you are reading is determined by how fast your lips can move! And like any habit, you can eliminate and get past it by consciously stopping your lips when you are reading.

2. Sub-vocalization

Sub-vocalization is an undesirable effect of the phonetic method as well. As a child progresses in his ability to speak, he is taught to do it silently within himself. Unfortunately, we tend to do this when we are reading as well. Hence, the speed you are reading is dependent upon how fast the voice in you is talking. This greatly impairs the speed at which you are capable of reading. Instead of having sub-vocalization impairing your reading speed, you can sub-vocalize on keywords with 'louder' volume in your head, but not every word. This will aid you in remembering as those keywords will stand out from the rest.

3. Regression and Back-Skipping

Another factor that hampers a person's reading speed is returning back to reading words and phrases that you have just read consciously or unconsciously. Regression is a conscious act where a reader goes back to read the same words. Such a habit is usually the result of fear of missing or misunderstanding the things he read and highlights his lack of confidence in reading.

Back-skipping is an act when the reader unconsciously skips back to words he has read.

Both are simply habits and can be reduced by forcing oneself not to repeat reading the sections he had just read thereby increasing his reading speed.

4. Taking in too few words per fixation

As mentioned earlier, your eyes move in 'jumps'. Each jump is a fixation. Poor readers take in 1 word per fixation which is extremely bad for reading fast. Most people are able to read 3-4 words in one fixation. Hence, to read faster, you have to increase the number of words you read per fixation. For starters, begin by reading 3-4 words per fixation if you are reading word by word. And slowly, increase it to 5-7, then 8-9 words per fixation in order to read at 600 words per minute and above.

You Can Start Reading <u>FASTER</u> Now By Applying Power Reading Techniques

The time has come now to know the actual helpful reading habit. Now that you are aware of the theory behind power reading and the poor reading habits, you have to eliminate the unwanted. Here are some techniques that you can immediately put into action and CONSISTENTLY increase your reading speed and comprehension!

1. Use a Pencil to Guide The Eye

Some people easily get distracted when reading. Hence, one of the techniques you can use to focus your brain and at the same time increase your reading speed is to use a pencil to guide the eye. To do this, simply place your pencil underneath the line you are reading and gently move it along as you read. To increase your speed of reading, move your pencil slightly faster than your normal reading speed to get your brain used to the new speed.

2. Look out for key ideas and circle keywords

The objective of power reading is to extract keywords. Thus while you speed read across the text, circle the keywords with your pencil. Vary your reading speed and slow down when the particular text contains many key ideas. Circle the keywords and continue to speed read after that. Hence, it is important to preview the text beforehand so that you know when to slow down and when to speed up.

3. Increase the number of words per fixation

By reading another 2 more words per fixation is sufficient to accelerate your reading speed to the next level. Frequent readers are able to read about 6-7 words per fixation, which is about 3 words more per fixation for someone who is not a frequent reader. My view point is that practice gets you there. Make it a conscious effort to read 6-7 words per fixation the next time you read your course materials. In fact, if you are determined to be a Power Reader, grab any book now and start applying what you have learnt.

4. Read with High Tempo Music at the Background

If you find reading at a higher speed uncomfortable at the start, play high tempo music when you are reading. Make sure the music has no lyrics or you would find yourself having 2 sets of words jamming your brain.

The speed you are reading will tend to match the tempo of the music. You will start to read faster and at the same time, music keeps your creative right brain occupied which will increase your concentration and minimize distraction.

Making this Power Reading Strategy a Habit

What you have now is the entire blueprint to power reading! Some of you may be excited about applying it immediately while some may feel overwhelmed with what you have just read!

Whatever be it, I advice you to apply these strategies IMMEDIATELY or at least the following day. Mere Knowledge is not power. Applied knowledge is POWER!

The information I have presented should give you an advantage among your peers. You now have the 1st Learning Strategy of the 'A' student.

Now what remains is to push your-self out of your comfort zone. Applying power reading for the first time would be TOUGH! The only way to make this strategy a habit is to keep applying it into your reading, overload your brain. After lot of practice, your brain will get used to it and power reading will flow as smooth as satin.

Remember, unless you take the effort to practice repeatedly, power reading will not be effective for you. Your desire and effort will determine your result. To have a 50%, 100% or even 200% comprehension or speed depends on YOU.

So set your POWER READING GOALS now.

Goal Setting Exercise

My Power Reading Goals Are:

Comprehension–> _____%

Speed–> _____%

Keyword Identification and Harvesting–> _____%

I will work _____ min/hrs daily for the next _____ days to achieve these goals.

You should have no problem reading the huge amount of stuff. Now after you have finished reading, it's time for taking notes effectively in a fun and interesting way.

CHAPTER 4
SIR, I HAVE A QUESTION!

Asking questions can be an accelerated learning strategy.

We use questions every day. Most of our daily conversation involves either asking or answering questions. Asking question helps the students to learn and be directed for what they are to do and how they are to do it.

It focuses on the student outcomes, including achievement, retention, and level of student participation. Posing questions before reading and studying material is very effective for students.

Questions can help students to make connections between what they know and what they are seeking to learn. They begin or continue discussion in addition they pinpoint and clarify issues to gather significant information.

> **Questions can help you to make connections between what you know and what you are seeking to learn.**

It promotes high level thinking and draws out what students are thinking. It is an opportunity to enhance the understanding.

Questioning is essential for two- way communication between a teacher and student, or between students themselves.

It increases the flexibility of teacher's responses, with teachers listening more and engaging students in more discussions.

Additionally, it enhances variety of questions asked by teachers. Questioning can be a tremendously effective way to teach and the most often used teaching techniques. Questions should play an important role in every classroom--both student questions and teacher questions.

Questioning also encourage participation among the students. It has a deep implication for the way that the student receives and process information presented and discussed in class.

It helps to stimulate thinking, assess student's progress, check on teacher clarity, motivate students to pay attention, provide repetition, emphasize key points, and lot more things to add to the list.

Asking questions causes the student to apply that comprehension to a new setting. It is an important way to increase the student's learning. Just as importantly, it is a way to force students to think during class.

Asking questions helps students to explore their available options and to evaluate progress. It exercises students in various levels of difficulty, draws solutions and awakens curiosity.

Moreover it stimulates interest in what they feel and think and help students to learn from each other and to respect and evaluate each other's contribution.

Well, in a nutshell let me explain why *'asking questions can be an accelerated learning strategy.'*

- Help students to identify their goals and purposes.

- Lead students to understanding and encourage them to talk constructively and on-task.

- Encourage the student's ability to solve a problem.

- Encourage students to thinking aloud and build confidence and independence in problem solving.

- Allow the students to anticipate probable outcomes of various choices and help to verbalize knowledge.

The difference between 'asking' and 'not asking' questions:

As students, by asking questions the effects and benefits are many. It would help them to succeed not only in the academic life but personal life as well. Questioning portrays ones ability to respond easily to the situations and circumstances around them.

By understanding its importance it's advisable to use it wisely to increase its' effectiveness. This habit when well cultivated will lead one to great heights.

By asking questions the students are easily driven to get facts. They tend to be unaffected by what others think and can easily claim credit for their efforts. In addition, it helps one to build confidence to construct a cohesive and highly effective team.

By asking questions, the students can absorb information rapidly, get an insight to a problem and will have the ability to stimulate the search for solutions. Moreover, they can enhance their enthusiasm and zeal for the subject. Finally, questions would tune them to remain selfless, open-minded and a life-long learner.

On the other hand, by not asking questions the students remain uninformed of facts. They tend to become sensitive and quite conscious of what others think when they start asking questions.

In addition, it would result in them hardly claiming any credit and they always remain vulnerable and find it difficult to inspire teamwork and commitment. This tendency would exude them from getting the necessary information resulting in them always remaining ignorant and unaware of solutions and reality.

Moreover, they can hardly awaken the enthusiasm and zeal needed, eventually making one an introvert and a shy person.

Asking question is a thought process:

Questioning has a long and venerable history as an educational strategy. Few students may just be too shy to talk, some do not have the courage to utter that first word; few others may think that everyone else in the room is better prepared or smarter than they are and so they are afraid to speak up. But, remember when you speak up and ask questions you:

- Challenges assumptions,
- Expose contradictions, and
- Lead to new knowledge and wisdom.

Basically questions are aimed at getting information on a particular subject or to elicit an opinion. Asking good questions is productive, positive, fruitful, useful, creative practical, valuable and can get us what we want. It provides a roadmap for you to follow.

It helps connect with your communicator in a more meaningful way. Moreover, it helps the communicator to know you as an understanding and a competent person. You will be able to gather solutions to the problems by reducing mistakes and be able to plant your own ideas.

Research has established a positive relationship between the amount of instructional content covered and student achievement.

In this way the classes can cover more material, student interest will be maintained, and achievement levels will be higher.

Questions have a number of uses. 'Raising a question' may guide the questioner along an avenue of research. At the beginning of a session, questions help reinforce the learners' understanding of "where we are now."

Differences between effective and non-effective question:

Effective questions open the door to knowledge and understanding. They are powerful and thought provoking. The art of questioning lies in knowing which questions to ask when. Effective questions can help you discover new opportunities and find creative solutions to it. Efficient questions are logical questions which inspire and motivate one to portray their talents and self-determination. They are always purpose driven and result –oriented. It reflects one's observations and shows the outstanding individual performance.

The quality of communication is influenced by the choice of words in which the sender encodes a message. Because all we all know the effective communication is a symbolic representation of a phenomenon.

Meaning has to be given to the words one uses as its merits are many. On the contrary if there's no meaning in your questions, then it's considered to ineffective with its demerits being many.

Ineffective questions are illogical questions which hardly motivates others, showing the individuals inefficiency and negligence. They can hardly be purpose driven and are not result-oriented as well. It shows the inattentiveness and the casualness of the individual. Moreover these questions lead to self-assumption and contradiction of facts making the questions seem vague and indistinct.

The benefits of asking questions:

Asking questions is a skill in itself. It involves a number of specific strengths. Questioning taps basic human needs-to improve, to compete, to be accurate because people always want to be competent. It is always an appreciated fact and motivates people to improve.

Questions help break the monotony of explanation and a break from listening.

> 1. To develop interest and to become actively involved in lessons.
> 2. To develop critical thinking skills and inquiring attitudes.
> 3. To review and summarize previous lessons.
> 4. To assess achievement of instructional goals and objectives.
> 5. To pursue more knowledge and wisdom.

Sitting and listening for extended period's leads to inattention.

Thus questions draw a participant's mind back to the topic.

Frequently asking questions during class discussions is positively related to learning facts.

It focuses student attention resulting in better comprehension. Oral questions posed during classroom recitations are more effective in encouraging learning than are written questions.

The young children and poor readers tend to focus only on elements that will help them answer questions if these are posed before the lesson is presented. Performance would be better on tests and exams

And no, of course you needn't stop to question anything and everything. Selectively is essential, and before you know it, your mind will seek out only the things that are of importance to you.

WHEN AND HOW TO ASK EFFECTIVE QUESTIONS

A question engages or encourages students to actively participate in a lesson and allows the students to express their thoughts and exchange information offered by their peers,
Questions are also used to keep students alert or on task during class time.

How you ask questions is very important in establishing a basis for effective communication. Ask questions which focus on the salient elements in the lesson.

If you could wave a magic wand and get every piece of information you want, what would you want to know? The answer will help you to pose the right question. Effective learning questions can serve as a starting point for the adaptation of learning.

Firstly to ask good questions one has to identify the type of questions he/she is currently asking, why one is asking them, and finally, what techniques can one utilize to improve the questioning that occurs in the classrooms.

When asking effective questions, it is important to wait for the answer and not provide the answer.

Questions should be planned in a logical sequence and should contain more requests for information than opinions. Phrase each question to maximize the amount of information you receive and make sure it contains fewer statements of disagreement.

If possible predict all possible answers and prepare a smooth transition from each possible answer. Have a good understanding of the fact because with an incomplete understanding of the problem it is very easy to jump to wrong conclusions.

- Be sure each question is necessary.

- Questions should invite the prospect to expand or clarify any point of disagreement and get the prospect to see things from your perspective

- Questions should narrow down generalizations and clears ambiguities. Avoid vague or critical responses.

- Ask a specific questions if you want to hear a specific answer.

- Avoid accusing, sarcastic or threatening language or tone in your questions.

Open-ended questions:

You can ask open-ended questions that elicit a wide rage of answers. Open ended questions do not invite any particular answer, but open up discussion or elicit a wide range of answers for creative problem solving.

It allows the prospect to move in any direction that is these questions are those that cannot be answered with a straight "yes" or "no." Open – ended questions ordinarily begin with Who, What, Where, When, Why or How to discover the roots of the problem. These questions can make people defensive, so be thoughtful in your use of them.

Closed questions:

Closed questions on the other hand are specific and usually answered with a yes or no, or with details as appropriate. This maintains control by directing flow of conversation

Focus:

It's advisable to always focus the discussion on the information needed. This would help you and the prospect to be 'in topic.' You can also improve your questions effectively by maintain eye-contact: This includes certain aspects like nodding in agreement, making statements and questioning in acknowledging the speaker.

Understanding:

To ask questions you first need to understand the topic. Just to make sure your understanding is correct you can restate briefly what the communicator had explained. On doing this you can confirm your understanding and in addition question what you want to know.

One must be open and willing to learn, even from what some people might consider a failure. Whether or not you are asking the right questions can have a huge impact on your success. Remember; how questions are asked and answered have broader implications than mastering content.

THE CONCEPT OF APPLYING QUESTIONS

As and always the concept of applying question is an art in itself which can be practiced in due course. In this chapter there are few examples for the concept of applying questions. Do remember, when you master the art of asking smart, meaningful questions, you not only make an excellent impression, but also improve the performance.

You can use the services of these six honest
men. Six honest men..? Who are they?
Well, take a glimpse of the following short poem by Rudyard Kipling. Whenever you're in a dilemma as to what to ask, just remember this short poem.

I keep six honest serving men
(They taught me all I knew);
their names are what and why and when
and how and where and who.

The following is a *brief description* about how you can use the questions: what, why, when, how, where and who.

'What' seeks the response of a noun or a verb that calls for action...
Examples:
What are you doing?
What is the solution?

'Why' seeks cause-and-effect.
Examples:
Why are you crying?
Why didn't you do it?

'When' seeks location in time or may also seek duration or a period of time.
Examples:
When can you come?
When will you finish?

'How' seeks the verbs of process and for quantity as well.
Examples:
How can this
happen? How can
you do it?
How much does this cost?

'Where' seeks the location of an action or event such as on, above, under, below.
Examples:
Where is it?
Where can I meet you?

'Who' connects people with actions and things...
Examples:
Who are you?
Who did it?

There is great value in the student exploring the problem and possible solutions. Effective questions stimulate, guide, and empower students to think critically. It's not enough just to ask questions but understanding which questions to ask and how to ask is what gets you results.

Let me give you another example of how you can question on some particular aspect. For example, the class is about APJ Abdul Kalam's book, "Ignited Minds," even before the teacher can start of with the presentation you can analyze and question the prospect.

Before giving the examples let me give you a brief description about this book. This is written by the President of India, Dr. Abdul Kalam, who explains about the "can do" approach of achieving greatness in the near future.

It is a true patriot's self-help guide to a better nation. It's aimed to fire the young minds to realize the dreams of a truly good life. He is not only the President of a nation but one of India's distinguished scientists, who was responsible for the development of India's first satellite launch vehicle. Now talking this book as an instance let me give you few examples of how you can question.

What does the title mean?
Is it an autobiography or a book on self-improvement?
How Dr.Kalam influence the individuals?
Is this book for the patriotic or just anyone?
What is the effect on the students?
What questions do you have about this book?
Have you read anything else by the author, if yes you can question about the similarities and differences between this book and the author's other books? In what way is it important to the students?
What can you learn from what the author says?

As you read the presentation you can question about the important sections or chapters of the book.

How does the book keep you going?
Can you relate any part of the section to an incident or event in your life?

When you finish the book you can predict your views or enquire such as:

Were your predictions on the book correct?
In what way did the book interest you?
You can question about the ways it's going to help you in your development?
What are the other facts that could be included or the details that could be omitted?
What according to you is the most interesting feature of the book?
In what ways can you relate to the facts and characters?
How does the fact contribute to the improvement of a nation as a whole?
You can also question about the author's writing style, imagery, dialogue title etc.
What questions you have for the author?
Would you recommend this book to the others?

The above are just a few examples. You can question a lot more on different issues. As far as the questions are relevant in their own aspect you can carry on with your enquiries.

An effective question is phrased in an open-ended fashion that does not suggest a particular answer and warrants a response of more than just a few words. Questioning clarifies our goals and helps to guide us from a state of confusion. The dialogue that effective questioning initiates also increases the number and quality of interactions within a class making it makes it more effective.

QUESTIONING TO SOLVE PROBLEMS

You can solve problems and clear confusion with the right kind of questions. Here are few ways about how you can go about doing it.

Probing:

Sometimes when answers to specific questions are not clear you can adopt the method of probing. Probing means getting deeper and deeper. It is positively related to achievement when it is clearly focused, e.g., on the clarity, accuracy etc.

Questions should be used fairly as a goal for your understanding. When your questions are thought-provoking it makes you more aware of the learning process. Effective use of probing is one of the most important questioning skills especially when you're a little confused.

Probing is the use of further questions to force the student to put together his or her partial knowledge into a more complete answer. Even a simple recall question may lead to important new learning on the part of the students if probing is used effectively. It often involves the use of follow-on or leading questions.

You can probe your prospect in order to supply additional information and to have more inclusive answers. Probing questions force the individual to think more thoroughly about the initial response.

- Follow up on a response.

- The question 'why' if not properly asked often cause individuals to become more defensive.

- If your question contains several questions, you may confuse the communicator.

- Analyze if your questions help reveal or clear up misconceptions.

- Behind every question there must be an intention to know.

Who? When? What? Where? Why? How? : They are all probing questions that can help you dig down into further detail.

Asking more questions:

Understand the difference between probing and asking for more questions. Asking more questions is designed to focus on the best solution.

When we allow for expansive thinking about a situation, it helps to draw the focus to the most relevant issues reflected in the subject.

Guess:

To guess and check is one of the simplest strategies. As we all know anyone can guess an answer. If the students can also check that the guess fits the conditions of the problem, then they have mastered 'guess and check.' When students are completely stuck, guessing and checking will provide a useful way to start and explore a problem.

Hopefully that exploration will lead to a more efficient strategy and then to a solution. While 'guess and check' can be used as one strategy the next one is to 'guess and improve.'

Guess and improve is slightly more refined and complicated than guess and check. The idea is that you use your first incorrect guess to make an improved next guess. It is often fairly easy to see how to improve the last guess.

Generate open-ended, expansive questions:

Open-ended questions as we know invite a number of potentially diverse responses. The question should have reason, focus, and clarity and must stimulate thought. The objective at this stage is simply to generate questions, not to answer them.

To that end, it is very important to put aside any thoughts about the fix, to resist answering questions, and stay open to new perspectives and ideas. It is generally a good idea to get input from the staff involved.

Ensuring that their answers remain anonymous will encourage student's responses. It is especially important to remain curious, to really listen. Any and all answers are good answers.

You should never say, "I don't know" as your final response:

'I don't know,' is basically being ignorant. Ignorance is lack of knowledge about a thing in a being capable of knowing. It is in fact the outcome of the limitations of one's intellect ability.

In other words it is the absence of information which one is required to have. The phrase, 'I don't know,' reflects your inability, attitude, approach, outlook, failure, capacity and the mind-set that you're capability is limited.

Remember, giving incorrect answers are fine as long as there are not totally irrelevant. After all, questioning and answering is a learning process. So, do attempt to answer the questions. Your teacher would definitely appreciate you for this attempt. Never utter, 'I don't know.' Once you adapt the ability of questioning and answering your mind will automatically work in tune with the process.

7 FATAL MISTAKES
WHILE ASKING QUESTIONS

1. Make sure each question is relevant:

It is necessary to think before you could ask a question. When your question is irrelevant it annoys the teacher and the students. Moreover, it shows your poor ability to understand and grasp the subject. So think before you ask a question. Thinking is about being systematic and keeping track and it also means following an idea for a while to see where it leads, rather than chasing lots of possible ideas. Students have to know where they have been and where they are going or they will get hopelessly muddled.

2. Questions should be clear of vagueness and ambiguities:

Ambiguities and vagueness most of the time irritate other people. When you're vague it shows that you're not clear and you yourself can't see what you're trying to express. You may get responses like, "Here's what I hear you saying. Is that right? One censor's his/her thoughts or assumes that things are already known. This can come out in vague words or statements.

3. The error of saying 'I don't know 'before asking or answering a question:

What we say is often severely abbreviated from what we intend or think. For example if you say "I don't know" it may indicate uncertainty or doubt. What don't they know?

How did they get to 'not knowing'? Avoid this phrase from your mental dictionary. If you are not clear about something, request the teacher to explain it more. As you get to know more facts about a subject you will have more and more doubts which can be asked in form of more questions. So never say, 'I don't know.'

4. Avoid accusing, sarcastic or threatening language or tone in your questions:

It is important to understand that your tone should not be harsh or unpleasant when questioning. Imagine yourself in the receiving end. Would you like to answer a question which seems threatening or harsh? Even if you reply, your answer will be with contempt and sometimes, the details would just be half the answer. Remember you get what you give. If your tone is inconsiderate you will also receive inconsiderate answers either directly or indirectly. So keep your tone and your questions neutral and unbiased.

5. Asking too general questions:

Strategically planned questioning will help you to form concepts and come to a conclusion. When you ask too general questions you are likely to sway away from the topic. This does not mean that you should not ask general questions but you need to be minimal and focus on the topic.

6. Behind every question there must be an intention to know:

You should not question just for the sake of doing it. But your questions should have a sincere and straight approach with a genuine effort to gain more wisdom and insight. After all, you question to know more facts and increase your knowledge. For this purpose to be solved you need to have an eagerness and purpose to learn. Hence behind every question there must be an intention to learn.

7. Not asking a question in the first place:

Well, there are many who just don't prefer asking questions for many reasons like the fear of ridicule, low self-esteem and many more factors. You should understand that there is no one is born with a mastermind but they take situations and circumstances at their stride and become genius.

Be curious. If Edison hadn't been curious about electricity we would have been staying in the dark. If Graham Bell hadn't been curious about transporting sound perhaps, we would have never come across something called a 'telephone.' So have an open mind and develop a curiosity to know facts.

LISTENING IS A PART OF EFFECTIVE QUESTIONING

When we look within the broader context of classroom interaction, how questions are asked has a tremendous impact on outcomes. These outcomes are shaped by how the students are encouraged to generate their own questions and how they build confidence.

Group discussions encourage active participation. Though asking questions is effective, it's not the only solution for a progressive growth. You need to listen attentively.

One needs to practice maintaining superior listening skills along with asking effective questions. When we really listen to a prospect, we begin to hear different levels of communication. This helps one to get to a deeper level of understanding, rather than coming up with an immediate answer. Listening actively is a key to more effective problem solving.

For effectively determining what the problem is, your best tools are active listening and questioning. Effective questioning requires it be combined with effective listening.

Remember, listening is a part of effective questioning.

- Active listeners are put aside other activities and are genuinely interested in the reply.

- Active listeners actively hear and receive the message openly.

- Active listeners are equipped to wait for answers.

- Active listeners are patient and are interested in the responses of others as they are in their own.

- Active listeners avoid prejudgment and are in tune with the social environment of the classroom as well as the facts and subject content.

By listening attentively you can also use that information to ask more effective questions. You can expand on this by articulating back to them about what you believe. This helps a person feel heard. By asking questions your prospect knows you're listening.

While in a group you need to provide time for the others to answer. This is an important aspect of listening. You need to wait for your peers to talk rather than talking for them which is very essential for an effective listener. You need to pay attention what the person who is talking is really saying. What is behind their words? Let go of your opinions so that they don't block you from learning more information.

By listening attentively you can gain understanding and wisdom. Moreover it allows the students to come up with their own solution or plans. Directly or indirectly the attention is on you: your thoughts, judgments, issues and conclusions. There is no room to let in the feelings of the person being "listened" to. You need to understand that you are being benefited!

Think as you listen and evaluate content. Don't be too keen on voicing your opinion. It's always advisable to be objective, achieve understanding and be committed. Reserve your thoughts until the other person stops speaking. Never interrupt or intrude other's personal space.

As an effective questioner it is important to listen without interrupting, waiting respectfully for each answer and considering it when it arrives before giving an opinion or launching into another question. Let your eyes not wander.

You should express your opinion but do not exaggerate or make a mountain out of a molehill. Avoid attempting to force or manipulate answers you want to hear. Thus you need to understand that behind effective questioning lies the ability to listen to the answer. Effective listening is a skill that requires nurturing and needs development. It's not a Herculean task. With a little bit of persistence and determination anyone can master the skill of listening.

CHAPTER 5

ACCELERATED LEARNING STRATEGY #2: TAKING NOTES WITH MIND MAPPING®

The Importance of Taking Notes

Hot on the heels behind Power reading is taking notes. I know what some of you are thinking... "Note taking is boring!", "Note taking doesn't work!" and some of you will even DOZE off when you write or read your notes!

Don't all of these sound familiar? You bet! I have been there and done that. And I know traditional note-making is not EFFECTIVE!

The system I am going to share with you is NOT making traditional linear notes! So stay with me. I will reveal to you 'A' student note-making tool in a few moments but before that, here is my answer to 'Must I really make notes?'

YES! Writing things down is the best way to remember something.

Research has shown that our brain is like a 'dry sponge', ready to absorb anything and everything that we experience!

Why is it then that we don't remember most of the things we hear see or learn when times passes? Remember the 'dry sponge' analogy? It is ready to absorb anything and everything. Hence at any instant, there are multiple objects fighting for the brain's attention! You are bombarded with numerous messages/signals in your brain at any given instant without your knowledge!

Hence, you have to make notes to retain this information for a longer period of time.

Which Category of Note-Making Student Do You Fall Into?

After observing hundreds of students and their note-making strategies, there are 3 distinct groups which I want you to be aware of. But only 1 out of these 3 groups has proven to score 'A' over and over again. Note-making strategies play a pivotal role in scoring As' for exams easily! It is NOT to be taken lightly. So let's have a look at the 3 categories!

Category 1 - The 'I don't take notes' students

Very often, these students refer to their textbooks very extensively which is extremely good at the beginning. However, as exams approach, referring to textbooks for information is NOT good for recalling and revision. Some clear signs of such students would be extensive 'highlighting' of keywords on the textbook with some scribbling at the side. (This is some form of keyword extraction).

The worst mistake someone can make is to highlight the entire text. And when I ask him why he does that, he replies confidently that everything is important and he will memorize word for word. Mind you, memorizing word for word is extremely time- consuming and ultimately leads to a mental block.

Category 2 – Students who take notes

These breed of students are wiser. They recognize the importance of note-making. There is a more concrete form of keyword extraction and a clearer structure of organized information to refer to. And this form of note-taking is the traditional linear notes.

Traditional linear note-making strategy is a popular strategy, which up to 90% of the students are actively using for their studies and exams. But a strategy that is widely used does not make it the best strategy. Sadly, the structure of linear notes does not actively engage the brain, which results in the reader finding it boring and has difficulty in memorizing it etc.

Would scoring an 'A' be possible with such a note-taking strategy?

Possible, if you are willing to put in lots of hard work, to the extent of sacrificing your social life.

The truth is that 'A' students utilize a more effective strategy. If you wonder why some 'A' students seem to do well without trying, read on.

Category 3 – note taking in a special way

So if 90% of the students use linear notes, what about the remaining 10%? Now, this is the 'winning' question that you should be asking.

Drum Rolls Please...

This 10% are the 'A' students who CONSISTENTLY get 'As' in their exams because they make whole brain notes!

Yes, that's right! Whole Brain Notes!

Whole brain notes cut short study time by as much as 85%. It allows you to compile all your notes into 1 piece of paper. You will have fun making and reading your notes. And have an easier time memorizing them. Now... this is what 'A' students have been doing under your nose!

Still wondering 'A' students seem to do well without trying? Read on.

What are Whole Brain Notes?

Before I can define what whole brain notes are, you will have to first understand how the brain works.

How does the brain work?

At a point in my life, when my grades were poor, learning was boring, parents and teachers were always screaming at me, I always hated those students, who were clever, more intelligent and often had good grades. And secretly deep down in my heart, I was jealous of them.

One question I always had in mind was, "how are they smarter than I am?" How do they always score better in class? Is it because they are intelligent or because they know the right strategies?

It was only after I did a lot of research that I realized that some of them are truly more intelligent than me, but there were also others who knew the strategies and skills to produce the excellent grades.

Sometimes you would hear that some gifted students are already studying in university at the age of 15. How can that happen? The fact that they are more intelligent than us is because they are nurtured from young to concentrate in the right direction.

There are some parents who actually trained their child from young. When the baby is in the womb, the parents already start to train the baby by allowing them to listen to classical music, eat healthy food, and talk to them in full complete sentences.

They avoided harmful things like television, alcohol, and many other things you can think of. The reason is that such habits can retard the child's brain from developing healthy.

And when the baby is born, they treat him or her like an adult, talking to them in full- complete sentences, and expose them everyday with new things to learn. And the baby is constantly listening to classical music.

These are some of the ways how some of the intelligent people are trained.

So can you be the same?

Perhaps at your age now, you can't be as good as someone who is trained from his baby days. But based on research, our intelligence can be put to good use if we use our WHOLE BRAIN.

First we need to understand how incredible our brain is.

Our brain actually contains 100 Billions of neurons or brain cells. Each cell in our brain is as good as a Pentium 4 processor, if not better. Each of these brain cells would serve a function in our body. That's why when people have stroke; part of their body is parlayed because the brain cells are affected. Without these brain cells, certain parts of our body will not function properly.

I would like to ask you how much of our brain do we use in our life time.

The fact about our brain usage is that most people hardly ever use more than 1% of the brain. And geniuses like Albert Einstein only used 3-4% of the brain.

If we can tap the potential of the rest of our brain, it means that we can be more intelligent than anyone else on the earth. But let's get back to the topic.

What's the difference between a genius and an average person?

The difference between a genius and an average person is that the genius uses more of his brain while an average person uses lesser as compared.

The brain is divided into 4 parts, but here, we are concerned with the left and right side of the brain. Both sides of the brain serve different function from one another. Let's take a look at how are they different.

Left side of brain - analysis, logic, math, sequence, linear and language
Right side of brain - emotions, creativity, color, rhythm, imagination and dimension

Most of us use one part of our brain as a result of the education system. In fact the subjects in the school often make us use one side of our brain. For instance for subjects like math, physics, chemistry etc, we are always using the left side of the brain.

The right side of our brain would be left with nothing to do. In fact, it often distracts us like humming music, tapping fingers and daydreaming when we are studying for our exams.

What would the genius do?

They use both sides of their brain for learning. Geniuses like Leonardo da Vinci and Albert Einstein used both sides of their brain and that is why they are still revered for their unusual talent.

What can you do to increase your level of intelligence?

Right now, you can start by trying to use your whole brain instead of one in all your subjects and you will see your results improving. For things like memorizing and taking notes, you can use your whole brain to make it more effective.

But first we will cover mind map.

Why do we use mind map® instead of linear notes?

Compared to linear notes, mind map is more of fun, looks better, and helps you absorb materials better in your studies. But the most important thing is it uses your whole brain instead of just using your left brain. Instead of allowing the right brain to distract you, why not work with it to help you in your studies!!!!! Good idea, isn't it?

Mind maps use both sides of the brain to make notes. From the right brain, it uses creativity, color and imagination. Instead of just using the left brain, now it's time to use the both brains.

From my experience, if it weren't for mind map, I wouldn't have even scored an A. Because mind map actually helped me memorize more effectively, understand the concepts more clearly, my grades shot up to As'.

The secret about mind map which many students don't understand is it forces you to comprehend and understand what you are studying. In mind map you cannot memorize word to word. You require understanding the whole passage or the concepts before you can draw it in your mind map.

Because you took more time and effort in understanding and drawing the mind map at first, it is but natural that you recall it more clearly and quickly. Besides, with more colors and pictures, your mind would naturally love the mind map more than linear notes, making it easier for you to register the mind map into your brain.

Many students give up the idea of doing a mind map citing lame excuses mainly because they are the ones who give up and despair easily when faced with difficulties. I strongly agree that starting a mind map is difficult, but as you continue to increase your creativity, it gets easier. Unfortunately most students can't pass the first step. Too bad for them.

What's so bad about linear notes then?

First, it does not make use of your whole brain. You can simply just copy it word to word from your notes. It won't help your brain understand what you have been taught.

Another reason is it is BORING.

The third reason is it's not HOLISTIC. One of the most important factors in learning is to see the bird's eye view of the topics you have learnt, and then to understand it in the big picture.

So back to the question, "What are whole brain notes"?

Simple. In fact, majority of you should have been exposed to whole brain notes at least once. But my guess is that many of you would have avoided it as you considered whole brain notes 'tedious', 'not necessary' or even 'childlike'. Now, the first step to scoring As' before doing anything is to have an open mind.

So here are some types of **whole-brain notes** you would have seen.

1. **Mind Map**
2. **Cluster Map**
3. **Time Line**
4. **Flow Charts/Concept Maps**

You are exposed to them even before reading this book. They exist in your textbooks and course materials. If a picture paints a thousand words, whole brain notes are capable of painting ten thousand words.

Wouldn't that free you lots of time for other activities? Definitely

And for the purpose of learning whole brain notes, mind mapping skill will be discussed and explained later.

Never Confuse Efforts with Results

Student A-Whole Brain Notes
Better Comprehension & Understanding
All the essentials in one page
Take Less Time to memorize a chapter

Student B-Linear Notes
Takes a longer time comprehension
Refer to a bulk of notes
Take hours to memorize

Fact: Majority of the student's are aware of the many benefits of whole brain notes but do not take any concrete action to apply them in their lives.

My advice to you is Never EVER get confused with efforts and results.

1 hour's work of making whole brain notes results in

1. Higher rate of comprehension

2. Essential points compiled in one page as compared to a bulk of notes

3. Needs less time to memorize Some efforts to reap greater results –

An 'A' student learns how to study hard but also smart.

Shouldn't you be using your note-taking time to do up whole brain notes and not linear notes?

Are You Still Making Boring, Linear Notes?

IF YES, make the decision to stop now! And start learning how to make whole brain notes.

How to Mind Map®?
A Step-by-step Blueprint to Making You
A Mind Mapping® 'A' Student!

Rules and Guidelines

1. Draw a main picture (IDEA) at the center of a horizontal piece of paper

- -use at least 3 colors

- -picture size at least the size of a thumb

- -don't use any frames

2. Create your sub-topic by adding a thick branch from the main picture.

- -CAPITAL Letters

- -Keywords focused

- -Words always on the line

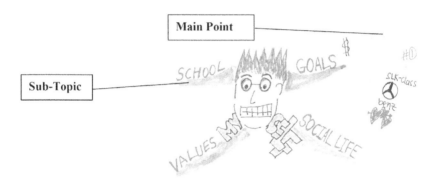

3. Developing your main points

- -branches radiating from sub-topic are small

- -one word per line

- -color of branches radiating from the same point should have the same color.

- -use keywords, symbols and images

4. Mapping out the details.

Some Other Whole Brain Notes

More Mind Maps®

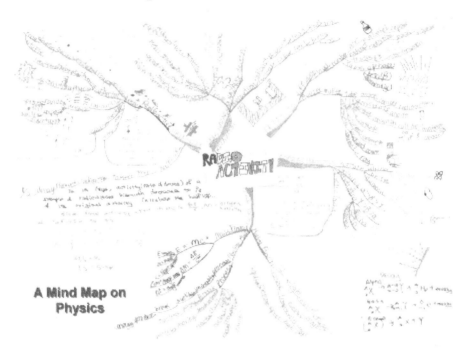

A Mind Map on Physics

A Mind Map on Chemistry

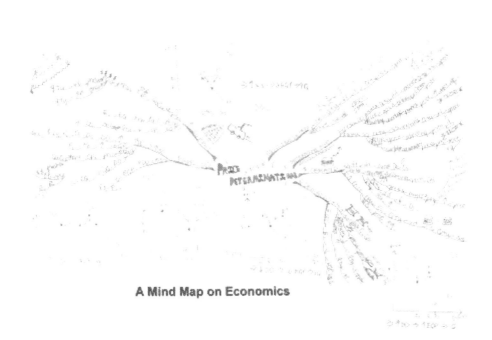

A Mind Map on Economics

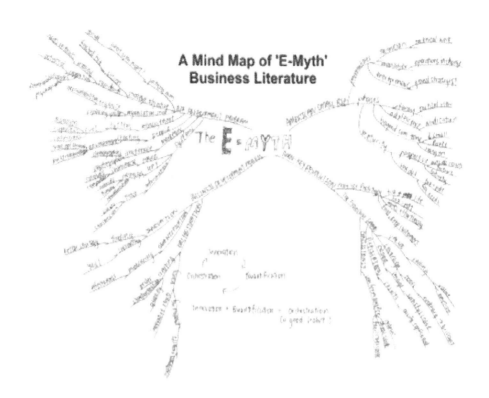

A Mind Map of 'E-Myth'
Business Literature

Concept Maps

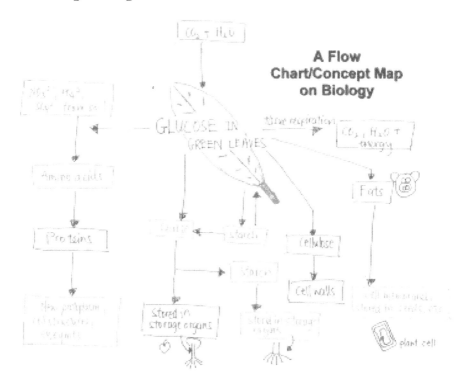

Cluster Maps

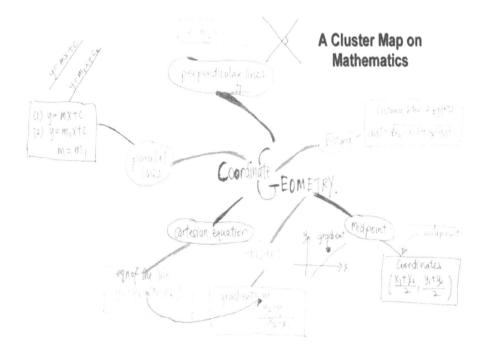

Timeline

CHAPTER 6
HOW TO MEMORIZE FAST AND
LASTING

PHOTOGRAPHIC MEMORY IN STUDIES

Having Trouble Memorizing For Your Test? Fear not...

When I don't know the right strategies for studying, I usually can't remember most of the things I studied. During the exams, besides not knowing how to do some of the questions, for most questions I can't remember what I have studied, especially for topics like geography and history. No matter how many times I read on the same paragraph over and over again the previous night, the next day when the exam starts, I can't remember a single thing.

And what I get for my results is always an 'F'.

Have you encountered this before!!

Some of you may have encountered this situation while some of you may have not.

Let me tell you something about the exams. What are exams created for? Exams are created to test the students whether they understand what they have been taught and whether they know how to apply what they have learnt.

So when you have scored well in the exams, it proves that you have mastered the subjects well. Many people have the misconception that when a student scores well for the exams, it means that they are gifted or they are clever. But the truth that they get good grades is because they understand the subjects well, are able to remember the information and apply it to different questions.

You know as well as I do that there are tons of concepts, equations and formulae you have to learn that might be asked in the exams. And to score well in the exams, you will need to regurgitate what you have memorized. Let's me share with you the secrets of having a SUPER GOOD MEMORY.

What is Memory?

If you look at a dictionary, most of them will say it's a process of recalling what has been learnt and retained. To remember something, we have to first **register** the information in our brain. And to **recall** means to **retrieve** the information that has been registered.

For example, you first read about octopus that it has 8 legs. Then you go to bed to take a nap. After you wake up and your mum asks you how many legs octopus has, you have realized you don't remember.

Did you forget?

No! You simply can't recall or remember the number of legs. But when you read again, do you go "oh I remember!"? The actual fact is the information is still in your brain, but you only can't recall the information.

And if that's the case, everything you see, hear and feel everyday in your life, it's somewhere in your brain whether you can remember it or not. Information is retained in your brain, but the only problem here is whether you can recall or retrieve the information in your brain.

Just like a computer...

Your brain is just like a computer. Whatever you see, hear or feel is saved somewhere in this computer. When more and more things are being saved, the place starts to get big and messy. If you are looking for something, it will be harder for you to find when you have tons of information saved in your computer.

Especially when they are similar types of files, it'll be harder for you to differentiate between the files and retrieving them would take a longer time.

What if you classified each of the files into different folder, differentiating each files with the other and making sure that they are labeled properly? Wouldn't this be easier for you to find the files you want?

So just like a computer, your memory will improve tremendously when you classify and arrange the information into well-classified folders. You can do the same to your memory by developing memory systems so that you can recall the information quickly in the exams.

How do you usually recall?

Let us try this question, "What did you eat for dinner yesterday?"

How do you recall what you ate yesterday?

How would I recall for example. First I would try to recollect what day was yesterday? Suppose that it was a Wednesday. And what did I do? I had been to teach a student math and it ended at 6pm. Then I went home to eat the rice, eggs and vegetables my dad had cooked for me.

As you can see, the way people normally remember previous incidents is by linking several incidents together. In my case, I had to go all the way to remember what happened at the start of the day, and slowly linked to what had actually happened by the end of the day.

In order for you to remember something new, you have to link to something that is in your brain already.

The difference between a good and a bad memory is the strength of the linkages. What do I mean by the strength of the linkages?

Let me give you another example, "how much can you remember of your younger days?"

I can remember how I fell down from my bike and hurt myself. I can remember how my roller blade gave way and I had a bad fall.

How about your first kiss? Who did you kiss and when was it? I can surely remember but I'm not going to tell you that ;)

How can I remember all these that happened a few years back? It's because there are strong linkages to them. The strong linkages are the pain I felt from falling and the excitement and happiness from the first kiss.

Do you now know why you can remember some of the things easily while you forget some? It's all about the linkages formed in your brain and how important they were in shaping your life at the point when you experienced them.

How can you create strong linkages?

1. Emotions
The strongest linkage is emotion. Which show would you remember more, a romantic movie where you were so touched that tears rolled down from your face or a boring movie that put you to sleep?

The reason why you can remember the movies is because it moved you, it touched your heart and it triggered some of your emotions.

The effective way to memorize is to use your emotions in what you are studying. It is especially effective if you applied it to all the subjects your intended to study.

At the same time you can create stories that arouse strong emotions. For example, if you are studying about the history of Japanese occupations, you can imagine you are one of the victims in the Japanese occupations and you are being tortured by them. The more emotions you can associate with it, the easier you can remember. But don't let that go too far that you get too emotionally attached and that affects your overall well being. Have a balance.

2. Visual Images
One of the most powerful memory techniques is to remember words using pictures and images. In reality, you can easily remember who you saw, what you see when you are walking down the street, whereas you can't remember most of the words you read in a book. You can perhaps only remember the images you imagine in your mind when reading the book.

Memorizing the whole chunk of words in your subjects would be impossible if you did not use any pictures. But if you translate the words into pictures, you will tend to remember the pictures more easily. Therefore, when you are studying, translate the words into images and pictures so you can remember easily.

3. Association
Association is also know as linkages which connects your memory together. In my opinion this is the most important technique in memorization. It is connecting the new fact with something you already know. By connecting with something you already know and when you want to recall, you would just need to remember how you link them together and you will remember the new fact easily.

4. Outstanding

Just like a computer, if I put the 2 similar files together in the same folder, how would you differentiate between the 2 files? It will be harder, right? So, if you are memorizing similar facts or information, how would you recall them?

How about if you are a teacher and you step into the class for the first time! Who would you remember? You will be sure to remember the student who is shooting a rubber band at you or creating havoc in the class.

Thus one of the memorizing strategies is making things stand apart from one another.

5. Humor/absurdity

Humor is another powerful trigger that can help you memorize things easier. You can use humor in making the linkages between the new facts and something you already know and so you can remember easily.

Absurdity helps you to memorize as well. By creating stories and linkages which may sound unrealistic and impossible in real life, it may make the linkages more interesting and fun and therefore you can recall it easier.

If I were to remember these words, "osmosis, photosynthesis, parachute, atomic bomb" in a humorous way, I'm going to create a story of my own.

Osmosis sounds like octopus and this octopus want to take a photo (photosynthesis) when he is sky-diving. But then as he was taking photo, he forgot to use his parachute and so he hit the ground like an atomic bomb killing many people.

Would it be easier to memorize these words by using the story above? Well, that was just an example and you could create your own stories. This helps you hone your creative skills as well.

6. Colors

One of the reasons why color is an important factor in memory is because it makes notes and words more outstanding than the others. Just like the paragraph above where the words are highlighted, you will be able to pay more attention to those words than the others. So instead of using just a single color, use multiple colors when you are doing mind map.

Moreover, it makes your note-taking more lively and entertaining instead of boring and monotonous.

7. Use your 5 senses

Instead of using just the eyes and the ears, make use of your 5 senses to memorize things. We tend to memorize things easier when we use our 5 senses to imagine. For instance, when you are imagining ice-cream, instead of just imagining what an ice-cream looks like, you should imagine you licking it, tasting the delicious flavor, the cold icy texture that triggers your senses and hear the "slurp" sound too.

Thus when memorizing, always do your best to use all the senses instead of 1 or 2.

8. Holistic

Holistic means to think in a whole. This means, you look at the whole picture, after looking at the bird's eye view of the subject you are studying. One of the ways to memorize it in a holistic view is asking yourself "why do you need to study the subject? What is the subject teaching you? And how does the particular concept or formula fit into the whole picture.

How Do You Use Them?

When you want to memorize new information and facts, what you should do is to form a linkage between information. And to memorize effectively use the above 8 important factors of memorizing to form powerful linkages.

Usually when you are studying for exams it is most often memorizing loads of information. So in order to memorize everything at one go, it's best to use the memorizing techniques above and link everything together.

Let's do a simple practice on memorizing.

Things to buy for Christmas

1. turkey

2. candles

3. Christmas tree

4. star

5. present

6. pizza

7. stockings

8. Xbox

Shall we practice using linkages to link everything together? So here we go.

First, visualize how during Christmas you are going to hold a big feast and so you decide to cook this yummy turkey and lay it on the table. The turkey suddenly stands up when you are about to slice it and it takes the candles threatening to burn Christmas tree. Then the star on top of the Christmas tree drops onto the turkey's head. The turkey is so frightened that it burns a big present where by suddenly the pizza man pops out of the present with the pizza on his hand. You quickly take a bite at the pizza and save the rest into the stockings before putting out the fire. But the fire is too strong and you have no choice but to take your HUGE Xbox to cover the fire. Without oxygen, the fire extinguish by itself in the Xbox.

Do you see how you can create stories by linking up the words? You can come up with a more creative one, different from mine. But how effective you can remember would depend on the 8 important factors and how you imagine it in your head. The more interesting, humorous and outstanding the story is, the easier to remember.

Take note that the way I've created that story is by:

1. absurdity ("A cooked turkey taking candles, threatening you that he will burn the trees")

2. humor ("the star dropping on turkey's head")

3. Outstanding ("the huge Xbox")

But at the same time, you will require to vividly imagine it in your mind with your 5 senses. Now you should be able to remember the Christmas list easily. Your turn!

I bet you can recall at least 6 or 7 from the list. Well Done! If you can't remember some of the words, it's probable that you are not using your imagination to create the images as playfully and effectively in your mind.

Not every word is easy to remember

Certain words in certain subjects are not easy to memorize because these words are impossible to convert into images unless you know or have seen them directly or indirectly. Words like photosynthesis, chromatography, and equilibrium are abstract words that you can't really visualize. What can you do then? You must still translate the words into an image or a picture and then link them together again with stories.

The first method you can use in handling such words is by using **the similar sound method.**

For the word 'photosynthesis', you can break down into 3 syllabus, photo-syn-thesis. So it sounds like photo-sin-thesis. You can imagine that taking photo anywhere in the bathroom is a sin.

How about chromatography? Chro-mato-graphy sounds like tomato giraffe. You can imagine a tomato monster eating up a giraffe. So when you think of the big tomato monster, you would be reminded of chromatography.

Do you get it? Now you need to practice.

1. Equilibrium -
2. potassium –
3. quantum -
4. isotopes -
5. nuclides –

Remember that there isn't any right or wrong answers. It is up to your own creativity to decide what the best substitution in the given situation is.

Here are some possible ways you can use.

1. equilibrium – equal lily brain
2. potassium – potato sir
3. quantum – Quarter
4. isotopes – I sold tapes
5. nuclides – Nude clouds

Most students find it difficult at first to think of creative substitutes to link the words together. However, after putting enough effort into thinking of creative substitutes, it will become easier and easier for you.

Another method when you can't find any substitution that may sound the same is the "**WHAT COMES FIRST INTO YOUR MIND**" method.

There's a game that goes like this...

When I say a word "fire", then the other person has to say a word that he can associate with fire. So he would say something like "water", and then the next person would say "fish" and so on.

So how can you apply this technique to memorizing?

Let me give you an example, when I say the word amoeba, what first comes into your mind? A mole is what comes into my mind. Thus I would form a story of "a man with a BIG mole went into a bar to dance".

What word comes into your mind when you see these words?

1. Lactic
2. Picasso
3. Anaerobic
4. Apostasy
5. Dilapidation

After you have the first thing that comes into your mind, form a story to link them together. Once again, make sure you use all the 8 factors to make the story easier for you to remember.

Memorizing for your exams

How would you apply all of what I mentioned above into your studies?
Let's say for a chemistry exam I need to memorize the following chapter.

Kinetic theory assumptions:

1. Gas molecules occupy a tiny fraction of the container.

2. Distance from molecules to molecules is far. (wide apart)

3. Gas in constant motion

4. Collisions are perfectly elastic

5. Increase in temperature increase the average speed (speed proportional to temperature)

As you can see, I have picked out the keywords that emphasize the main point. There is no need for you to memorize the whole sentence but only the keywords which will give you the entire meaning of the sentence.

And then what you need to do is to translate the keywords into pictures.

1. tiny fraction → a rat is so small compared to an elephant.

2. wide apart → ballet dancer can spread their legs wide apart

3. constant motion → always pass motion

4. perfectly elastic → rubber band

5. speed proportional to temperature → superman can fly faster when you take a candle and burn on his backside.

What I have done first is to associate the keywords into some interesting story that is linked back to the keywords.

Secondly, I created the story with the Links.

The rat felt inferior because he was so small compared to the elephant so he cried his way into the ballet dancer's feet who shrieked and her legs split wide apart. She was so scared that she suddenly passed motion and in order to stop her from passing motion, you had to tie a big rubber band to her backside. You burnt a candle on the ballet dancer backside and she flew like a superman.

I have used the links and created a story that links all the links together, with a bit of humor, movement, absurdity, imagination, and many such principles in memory.

So now can you easily remember what the assumptions of the kinetic theory?

1.
2.
3.
4.
5.

Now you have learnt the basic about memorizing. It is about memorizing the important keynotes that you would need to know for exams.

How to memorize Mind map® effectively?

After you have drawn the mind map, it is now time to memorize the whole mind map. In exams, there should be no problem in answering almost all the theory questions.

First, you would need to start by looking at the macro level - memorizing the mind map from the bird's eye view. You can start by memorizing the Sub-heading, and then followed by the way it can branch out.

For instance, a certain picture shows you the main topic with 4 sub-heading of a mind map. You can recall easily by remembering that the topic "MYSELF" has 4 sub- headings. And you can form a story with the 4 sub-headings.

For example, in the recent world cup, after scoring a goal, the police went out to catch those people without a social life. They put them in a school to teach them the values of watching world cup and so they can make the world a better place to live.

I know this story is a bit crappy and crude. Of course this is not the best way but it's an example of making an absurd, "funny", ridiculous story in an entertaining way in the process of memorizing easily.

The idea here is to memorize the main content and the sub-heading first.
Next, you can apply the memorizing principles by linking all the branches into a story. This is known as the micro memorizing of the mind map.

From here, I would prefer to memorize those in the same branch for example.

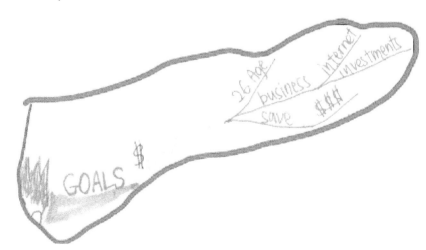

And I would form a story with this branch before I go into the next branch "dean's". In fact, it would be easier to memorize the first branch before you move over to the next branch. As it follows a system, it will be more effective. But how would I form a story?

I would say there was a millionaire who married a woman aged 26 and his business went 'BOOM' because she kissed him. He decided that he no longer wanted to work so hard and so he logged onto the internet to check his investments. He realized his investments were gone because the woman took them away. The money he saved for so long was all gone.

You would need some practice before you can be good at this. But after you memorize the mind map and whenever you revise, it's important for you to draw out the entire mind map, to check whether you can recall what you have memorized.

Memory pattern of the brain...

What is your memory pattern of your brain?

Even when you have the strongest linkages, the most hilarious story, used all the memory techniques that have been taught to you, would you be able to memorize the information if you never recall it for one month, 1 year, or 5 years? Would you still remember?

There's actually a pattern in memory that allows you to memorize things for the long term. Most of the students don't understand this memory pattern and therefore waste more effort in revision. The truth is, if you know the memory pattern and apply it, you can shorten your time in revision. Let's say a normal student would take 2 hours to revise his work. You can take as little as half an hour to be as good as him if you know the memory pattern.

So what is the memory pattern?

Research has shown that after you first absorbed something from what the teacher has taught in the class and if you don't revise what you have learnt 5 minutes after the class has ended, 80% of what you learnt would be lost by the 2nd day.

If you don't revise within the week, you would almost forget everything you learnt. And thus you would have to start from scratch again. That's why students always spend most of the time starting from scratch because they never revise what they have learnt the next day.

You can actually effectively reduce the amount of time by 1 quarter if you revise what you have learnt 5 minutes after that class. And then 1 day after you have been taught, and 1 week after you have taught, followed by 1 month, 2 month.

By then, if you have consistently revised your work, when you are studying for your exams, you would actually need just a little amount of time in revising, and you can spend most of the time practicing and still have time to relax and have fun.

The more you revise the lesser time you spend in revising the same topic in the next revision. What I am trying to say is that for the first revision you may take 1 hour, but the second revision would only take 45 minutes. And this time gap is bridged when the numbers of revisions increase.

That was exactly what happened to me when I was in 'A' level. I was consistently revising my work and when the exams approached, I actually had time to revise as well as relax. Unlike my other classmates, I was more relaxed and had no fear of performance.

What happens if you did not do this?

What most students would do is to start their revision about a week before their exams or some would start one month before their exams. Most have this mentality that since they would forget when they start revising early for their exams, they must as well start late so they can recall easier.

That's far from the truth. The truth is if they do this, most likely they have no time to memorize everything or practice the questions. They would feel the stress and pressure from the approaching exam date. And because of the stress and pressure, they can't memorize very well.

Because of that, they would also mix up some of the concepts and the understanding. If they are still confused with certain topics and subjects, they won't have the chance to clarify their questions.

And they would take more time to learn the concepts and fundamentals from scratch because they would in all likelihood have forgotten most of the stuff. Compared to those who have consistently revised their work, they would spend more time studying.

Let's take a look at what you do after memorizing everything.

CHAPTER 7

There was a time when I memorized everything in the mind map and I still scored a lousy C. I had no problem with memorizing all my formulae, memorizing all the words and definitions. But somehow when I looked at the questions, I wouldn't know which formula to use and how to solve the questions using the formula. There were also questions when I didn't know what was asked for and what type of answers would be appropriate for those questions.

It was then I realized that to get an 'A' I need something else. I would need something more than memorizing. I must master how to answer and apply what I have learnt and memorized.

In order to help you understand the importance of application, let us take a look at what the education system aims to achieve and the purpose of exams. In the past, exam questions were mostly theoretical and you could pass by just memorizing everything in the textbook.

In the present competitive world, the education system aims to help students achieve certain learning objectives so that they can survive in the tough competitive environment.

In any of the education systems, depending on the various subjects taught, the students are exposed to various concepts, formulae and equations. Therefore during exams, it is necessary for the teachers to know whether you have learnt and absorbed what was being taught in class and whether you know how to apply them to various questions, thereby testing various thinking skills.

With that in mind, you know as well as I do that students who truly understand the topics and practice what they have been taught, would eventually be the ones that scored well in the test or exams.

How can you do that?

As you can see, the education system requires you to understand what you have been taught, and in order to test that, your teachers or instructors would ask all types of questions to meet their **teaching/learning objectives**.

So first of all, to master the art of answering questions, you must know what the learning objectives are. In another words, what kind of knowledge the topic or subject introduces you to. And most important of all, what is the purpose behind learning that particular subject.

For example, when you are studying about gravitational law in Physics, you can ask yourself what this topic teaches you and what you can learn. With your objectives on this topic clear, you can roughly estimate the type of questions that can be asked in the exams.

List down all the formulae and concepts

When the subjects are taken into consideration, there's only a fixed number of ways how the test papers can be compiled. For example, when testing students on a particular formula, there are only a **fixed number of ways** the question(s) can be framed.

For instance, let's say you are talking about area of triangle using the formula area = ½ X breadth X height

There are only a fixed number of ways by which the exam papers can test you.

When they test you, they would actually give you 2 of the variables like the breadth and the height before they will ask for the area. Here is the number of ways they can test you on this formula.

Given Area and Breadth   Find Height

Given Area and Height   Find Breadth

Given Breadth and Height   Find Area

Besides testing you with just one formula, they could also test you with 2 or 3 or more formulae together in a question. So to find the answer, you will need to master the different type of formulae and how they work with each other.

Therefore you would need to list down all the formulae that you have been taught. Try to get all the past year questions and other school exam papers. In order that you master all the questions, it's essential that you take all the questions and classify them into the various formulae as above.

There would be some questions that will overlap one another.

Let me give you an example of how I did it when I handled my 'A' Levels.

For example I chose a topic called "Group 7 elements" in the subject "Chemistry".

At my level, I was required to know the similarities and trends in physical and chemical properties of chlorine, bromine and iodine.

9. Characteristics of physical properties

10. The relative reactivity of the elements as oxidizing agents

11. Some reactions of the halide ions

12. The manufacture of chlorine

13. The reactions of chlorine with aqueous sodium hydroxide

14. The important use of halogens and of halogen compounds

All of these are taken from the objectives of the notes I have. With that, I roughly had the idea of what was going to be tested.

Start Collecting Exam Papers

Next, I took the past year papers and looked at all the questions and classified them to the above objectives.

There were questions like 'find the reaction of group & elements when heated'. This comes under the category of similarities and trend in physical and chemical properties.

Some were testing on whether I know how to form the equations of the elements with other solutions like acids. So that was considered to be one type of questions that I had to master. Knowing how various Group 7 elements would react with various acids and the explanations for that would require that I memorize some important facts.

For example, one of the questions in the exams may look like this, "describe and explain the reactions of elements with hydrogen, and thermal stabilities of the resulting hydrides". I would actually classify this under halides and the reactions of halides.

What I am doing is classifying the questions into various learning objectives. In this way, I have a better understanding of the whole topic and I know the different number of ways the examiners can come out to test you on various concepts and learning objectives.

If you do what I did, such as classifying all the questions into various sections, and practicing the questions, you will be able to handle most types of questions. Of course there will be some difficult questions, but with most of the questions you will have no problem.

Practice and list down all the steps in doing the questions to get full marks

After listing the questions, you will be required to write down the necessary steps in doing the questions. For different questions, you will be tested on different formulas or concepts. Hence, you would need to provide different steps in order to get the right answers.

In addition, after you write down the steps, you will have a clearer picture of how the exams can test you. In fact, you will realize that the questions can't be too different in one way or another.

Here's an example for mathematics. For the lower level mathematics, there is a chapter on Decimals. The chapter teaches the basics of decimals, how to calculate (addition, multiply, subtract, division) the decimals, converting units etc.

I looked through the assessment books and test papers and found out the possible questions they will ask you about decimals.

1. Find the best estimates - rounding off questions
2. Conversion of units – converting liters to milliliters, grams to kilograms, meters to centimeters and so on.
3. subtraction, addition, multiplication and divisions of decimals
4. fraction to decimals or vice versa
5. fill in the equations for example 7.5 X 5 = + 20.4
6. problem sums

I actually classified my questions into the above type of questions. I would have taken everything out of the tests papers and classified them into various categories such as –

1. Qn 3, Qn 5, Qn 11
2. Qn 2, Qn 21, Qn 15
3. Qn 1,
4. Qn 4, Qn 6
5. Qn 10
6. Qn 22-30

With this, you can start practicing and be aware of your weak areas so that you can improve on it. You will also realize that by doing this, you are aware of what the exams are testing you about.

The Important Thinking Process

In order that you to score excellent grades, you are required to go through the thinking process. At first you may not know how to answer a single question, it may be a tedious process for you. But the crucial part is, after looking at the solutions, you must be able to **understand the solution**, and then do it by yourself.

Most students when faced with a difficult question would look for the answers without thinking. After you have consolidated the questions, it is important for you to think through the solutions and practice how to do it on other questions. Only then, you will be able to understand and tackle other questions.

How can you save time doing the questions?

After you have classified them into various categories, you will find that most of the questions fall into the same class of formulae or concepts. Now you don't need to do all the questions but would just need to do around 3 questions that test you on the similar questions. If you get all correct, you can carry on with other formulae, if not, continue with the same questions until you get it right and make sure you understand them before you carry on.

Most of the students waste their time doing the same questions over and over again and thinking they would do well in the exams. Can you imagine the time loss when you are doing the same type of questions over and over again? And the worse thing is you don't learn anything from doing the same questions over and over again.

Saving time in the long run

Some students say "isn't this going to waste a lot of time?" and some even say they don't have time to do this type of a grilling practice session. The truth why students don't have time to do this is because they leave everything to the last minute. They cram everything, study on the day before exams, and practice their questions before the exams. How would anyone have time if you are doing the last minute studying?

This method is going to save you most of the time. Because when you start doing your past year papers, you would know what is being tested and so you can actually avoid doing the same questions repeatedly.

Furthermore, you would understand the concepts and formulae very well because you can see the holistic view. You will also know when to apply the concepts and formulae to answer different types of questions. Even if the questions were twisted, you will actually know that the questions are more or less the same because you are being tested on the formulae that were taught.

CHAPTER 8
DISCUSS, PARTICIPATE, EXCEL!

Class discussions help students to examine, evaluate and share knowledge about a subject matter. It's always advisable to actively participate in the class for a number of good reasons. Participating in class gives you a lot on information, ideas and facts.

The rapport between the teacher and student increases:

What active participants do is allow the teacher and the students to seize on the 'teachable moment.' It also allows the teacher to respond to developing situations in such a way as to maximize opportunities for learning. The rapport between the teacher and the students can encourage participants to express their feelings fully and honestly.

When there is active participation you can share and generate your ideas. Moreover, it gives you good opportunities to ask questions and to help you understand or to hear others' views. They not only give insights into what other participants think, but also why they think it.

Developing skills and interests:

In actively participating in the class the students are able to develop their skill and understanding. The social nature of participating can enhance learning; develop group commitment and interpersonal skills such as listening and speaking.

When students consider themselves to be participant, they learn more and they take pride in what they learn because it helps the students to become personally involved in their education.

Moreover they become active participants in learning how, for instance to evaluate a theory and can gain confidence in their intellectual abilities. They can develop new interests and by varying the kind of discussion and the kinds of participation in class activities the needs of students are often served better.

Defeat conflict:

Constant participation also helps students to see conflict as a good thing and learn ways to disagree without being harmful. They can learn to first acknowledge and analyze before beginning their own critical analysis.

Listening:

Listening is yet another effective form of participating. Remember, your teacher is the one who actually prepares your question paper. So listening would also help you to have an idea about the question paper you'll receive.

Hence listen openly, fight distractions not just words. Most important do listen between the lines. Stay in active body state to aid listening. Be very clear in your mind about your goal.

If you have something to say don't interrupt, do listen patiently, wait for your turn and then ask. You can always write them down in a piece of paper and bring them up later. When you listen to what is being said you will be able to not only meet your needs but also help your peers to approach the right direction.

So realize the importance of participating in class and that listening plays a strong role in that.

The importance of participating in class should be made a priority if it is not already because without participation no real or effective work could ever be carried out. Do understand that it will help you to perform better in your exams and otherwise.

On the contrary when you neglect the importance of participation you can expect a lot of difficulties and problems. Thus understand the importance of participation and always work to enhance them.

In this way you can soar higher and higher!

THE IMPORTANCE OF GROUP DISCUSSIONS

To understand concepts:

'As iron sharpens iron so one man sharpens another'.
Proverbs 27:17

With group discussion the students can develop their skills and understandings which involving reasoning and problem-solving. They can understand concepts better. Group discussions are more effective environments for exploring, and possibly shaping, the values and attitudes of students.

To understand concepts better the students need to think and group discussions pave the way for students to think. If students are expected to learn to evaluate evidence and data, analyze or think critically, then the importance of participation in these discussions is a must.

To clear doubts:

With the group discussions there are various chances to clear doubts and uncertainties. It provides an in-depth view which is not attainable from individual questioning. They can clarify what they do not understand in a non-judgmental environment.

Apart from clearing doubts, unexpected ideas and new perspectives can be explored. And by easily building on each other's ideas and comments the students are able to synthesize several sources of information.

If there's something that that the student does not understand or if he/she does not already have a rehearsed answer, then it's recommended to use these opportunities to gain understanding or solve problems.

To verify if you are on the right track:

Students learn the most when they can take an active part in learning instead of being passive recipients of information. Life can be monotonous and boring if the students have to only listen to teaching and there are chances of them assuming things by their self.

Thus participating in the discussions would help them reveal if they are in the right track and what they have assumed is correct and exact. In addition, they can gain the others 'in-sight' on a particular topic which reflects their thought pattern. These insights would help the students have a better view of the suggested topic.

Exchange information:

All students inclusive of the ones, who are shy, get a chance to participate and exchange information in desirable ways. Group discussions enable one to draw on the ideas.

Students may work together on improving sentences and may brainstorm together on the development of facts and information. They can have meaningful discussions and exchange facts about how they fit what they are learning into their construct of the world.

Engaging in a two-way exchange lets them explore ideas rather than just answer questions. They provide an atmosphere for students to create view from different perspectives, improve their communication, expression skills and collaborative skills.

Being in the group is an enjoyable experience.

Group discussion gives you the experience of working in a team. It's easy to plan questions that automatically include everyone because the students are less intimidated as they are not answering as an individual, but as a group.

It can be especially valuable as it provides an excellent means to help students develop a working rapport. Working in a group has got a lot of advantages. It helps the students to build an effective team.

Each individual can practice the planning and monitoring skills they need, to become good individual problem solvers. Moreover, it is one of those effective methods where the leadership quality [which is very essential for students] can easily be developed.

HOW TO DO A GROUP DISCUSSION EFFECTIVELY

Apart from knowing the importance of group discussion, students should also be aware of how to do a group discussion effectively and efficiently. Your goal on a group discussion is to learn facts and gain wisdom, hence learning should be seen as a co- operative, rather than a competitive process. Here are few suggestions on how a group discussion can be resourceful one.

Improving personality traits:

Personality factors of individual students such as shyness, aggression, language problems can combine to undermine the individual. All these inhibitors have to be managed so that learning can be enhanced.

To overcome these inhibitors, one method is to practice reciting the details [you would like to talk about in the discussion] before a friend or a family member even before the discussion. In this way you can identify your faults as well as gain some confidence.

Well, these liabilities cannot be rectified overnight but as you practice your sure to achieve your goal. Build your confidence by making short contributions. Set yourself targets like making a contribution for a day.

Question yourself why you feel nervous and challenge your assumptions accepting that having your ideas challenged helps you learn.

Preparing beforehand:

First and foremost it is important to make sure that you have been well briefed about the topic and that the resources required to your contribution is available. You can incorporate statistics, quotes, and other support materials or include your own opinions too.

These will make all of the details more interesting! A good fact or opinion will keep everyone following along more to think about. Read more widely around the topic in advance. Prepare thoroughly and make notes beforehand on points you could make. You may even talk to other students or your tutor about the topic in advance.

Have a balance in your answers:

You may be given assignments to participate, either to start a message of your own, reply to a message of your instructor, or a classmate. The challenge is to do this without getting too long-winded! Don't agree with everything. When you agree with all topics in reflects your inefficiency to deal with facts. You can agree with the opinions by citing examples. It makes more sense that way.

On the other hand don't disagree with everything. You won't impress anyone by being critical of every fact and opinion. ! If it is critical, then it should be specific and clear for possible improvements. Make sure that there is a balance in your answers. Express what you like about their ideas or compliment their intentions.

Small groups:

By far, class students may form different small groups with their own circle. Small groups are more effective than larger ones because they provide an excellent situation in which all the students can actively participate and contribute ideas. In small groups students can lead discussion of their own passages. Sitting in a circle allows everyone to see and communicate with each other.

Don't get personal in a discussion.

Be generous in interpreting others. Always remember: *A gentle answer turns away wrath, but a harsh word stirs up anger. Proverbs 15:1.* If you encounter difficulties or the argument gets too hot, let your instructor know.

Never respond with ridicule or sarcasm and don't become too emotional with your answers. Before beginning your own critical analysis learn to first acknowledge and analyze what the person with whom you don't agree means. Always attempt to see conflict as a good thing and learn ways to disagree without being harmful.

In addition:

- Ask clarifying questions if you are not sure you understood. Asking more questions is the best sort of reply.

- Raise a hand when you'd like to speak

- Keep a reasonable voice level. Be clear and focused in your answers.

- Avoid a back and forth discussion between you and another peer.

- Make notes during the discussion on what others say or you might say.

- Avoid asking questions that you won't be able to act on.

- Try to respond positively to each student's comments.

- Learn to address not to persons or individuals but the issues.

- At the end of the discussions summarize or write a brief note about the discussion for future references.

- Finally, learn to make the most of it.

WORKING WITH A COMPANION

Working with a companion has its own advantages. You can be a source of encouragement for each other. You can be sure that there's someone you can rely on in times of distress apart from your parents and teachers. Now, here are few guidelines on how you can have a strong bonding with your companion.

Express your goals positively.

You and your companion can have set goals and work to achieve them. When one loses hope or goes off track the other can correct the person and bring him on track. This is the advantage of working with a companion.

Write down the goals to avoid confusion. Have a date and a time so that your achievement can be measured. By having set dates you not only know the exact goal to be achieved but you can also take satisfaction from having completely achieved it.

Set priority to each goal so that you can direct your attention to the most important ones. If you have too many goals to be achieved at a time, then you may end up doing nothing at all.

Let your goals be small and achievable. Remember, larger goals are derived from smaller ones. Do not be afraid of failure. Failures are stepping stones to success. See how you can improve from each experience and situation in life.

Set specific and realistic goals. Do have a clear and a realistic understanding of what you are trying to achieve. If your goals are specific and realistic you can be confident of achieving them. This would inspire you take up more challenges.

The Importance of Showing Appreciation:

Always make it a habit to appreciate each other. When we express appreciation we give them a sense of significance. It shows that his/ her accomplishments make a difference to you. Give them honest praise for their effort.

Examples: "Thank you for helping me on this essay."

"Thank you for accompanying me."

Do understand that when you appreciate a person, you need to do it sincerely and genuinely.

There is a saying which goes like, "If you want to feel good about yourself, make someone else feel good! It's as simple as that. A written compliment is also a good idea. If it's your companion's birthday, you probably can get a birthday card and write down all the points you appreciate in him/her. These small gestures will go a long way in keeping your relation strong and steady.

The importance of communication:

Effective communication is an essential component of success. The process of transmitting information from an individual to another is a process to master. The choice of words or language you use will influence the quality of communication.

A major source of problem in communication is defensiveness. When people feel threatened they will try to protect themselves; this is natural.

This defensiveness can take the form of aggression, anger or competitiveness. Thus it's advisable to try to make adjustments to compensate for the likely defensiveness.

Listen openly and with warmth to your companion. Listen and Respond in an interested way that shows you understand the problem and the other's concern. Learn to be patient and understanding. Avoid accusing and blaming the other.

CHAPTER 9
MANAGING YOUR TIME

How Do You Score A's With So Little Time?

I was amazed by how some of the top students in the school could study so well and yet have time to pick up playing instruments, and hold important positions in their CCA or in the school. How did they manage to score As' with so little time while I couldn't score any A even when I had so much time?

Everyone has the same amount of time. The top students have 24 hours a day and the weaker students have 24 hours as well. But why is it that they can do so well in their studies while having so many activities but the other students with more time to study, can't even score a single distinction.

What's the difference between the 2 types of students?

The answer is that the top students plan and organize their time very well, while the weak students are those who don't plan and organize their time well.

If you ask the top student what he plans his studies everyday, he would tell you the specific things he is going to study each day. He would tell you how much of his time are allocated to his studies. Sometimes, he has even started on the homework that would be due next week.

And if you ask a weak student what he is going to do for the day, he would say finish all the homework that is going to be handed next day. After finishing his homework, he would watch television or maybe play computer games.

How you use your time will determine the results you get

If you have a look at those people who are successful in their life, they are the ones who know how to organize and plan their time. They achieve most of their goals and are satisfied with their life. Look at the rest of the people and how they spend their time? Most of them waste their time on television shows, playing games, and pass their time doing nothing useful.

Most successful people treat time as money. In fact, when you ask them of their time, they would charge you as much as $1000/ hour depending on their expertise and career. That's how precious time is to them.

To you, time is important because you have limited time to absorb and learn all the subjects and topics you are required to study. If you invest your time in studies, you will gain much more than you would have gained in watching drama series or entertaining movies. (Unless you would want to be a movie director).

The worst mistakes that students commit is they don't know they are wasting most their time and they think they are using their time wisely.

So it is essential for you to write down the time you spend on a daily basis and check on how much time have you wasted in a week.

What is wasting time?

Wasting time is using more time than expected to do the necessary things like bathing, eating, resting and on many such activities. If you take more time than necessary, you would have lesser time for other activities that can help you to achieve your goals.

Time is also wasted if you are not spending on activities of your goal. That means you are not working towards your goals. It's crucial that you spend most of your time working on your goal. But most students waste their time on things like computer games and television.

Prioritizing your time

Another skill that you have to pick up is prioritizing your time. Because everyone have 24 hours a day, it's essential that you pay more attention on activities that are goal oriented.

Successful people know how to dedicate the miscellaneous activities to other people while spending most of their time on activities that are goal oriented.

Average people are dragged down by the daily routine of urgent but unimportant activities like watching television, playing computer games and going out shopping.

There are actually 4 categories that you can compile your activities into.

I	Important and urgent
	Homework
	Projects
	Surprise
	test
II	**Important but not urgent**
	Doing Mind Maps
	Daily
	revision of work
	Collecting and practicing questions
	Memorizing and recalling

III	Not important but urgent
	Answer Telephone calls,
	Checking emails,
	BGR relationship
IV	Not important and not urgent
	Playing arcade
	Surfing internet
	Reading magazines
	Doing nothing

Important and urgent (I)

Important and urgent are those activities that are goal-orientated and require us to complete as soon as possible. These activities are doing homework, finishing up the projects, studying for surprise tests and similar such activities.

Most of the time, when we procrastinate or delay spending time on activities such as homework, studying for tests, projects, assignments, there will be a snowball effect and we end up doing them the last minute. Thus they become very important and urgent.

The disadvantage of doing things last minute is that we may end up having no time to finish them, and it will cause us to be stressful and pressurized. In these types of situations, the efficiency for learning would be lowered and we will not take in as much as we would if we had done earlier.

To be out of the quadrant, we would need to plan our time ahead and organize what we are going to do each day. In addition, we would require completing the homework as soon as we are given the assignment. So we can allocate more time for other important but non-urgent stuff.

Important but not urgent (II)

Do you know why there are so few successful people in this world? It's because only the successful people would spend most of their time doing activities that are important and urgent.

Important but not urgent are activities which are also goal-orientated but not as urgent. For a successful student, activities such as recalling and revising daily, doing mind map, practicing on questions, doing homework and assignments in advance, start revision way ahead are examples of important but not urgent.

The advantage of doing this is to have a head start in understanding the subject well, and to have a stronger foundation than your peers. Learning this way will be more effective because there's less pressure and stress. You would have remembered the facts and information more clearly by this method.

Normally, after you finished the (I) important and urgent activities, it is a must for you to invest your time in these activities unless you don't want to score A's.

Not important but urgent (III)

These activities are not goal-directed but they are urgent. Activities such as answering phone calls, checking e-mails, watching your favorite shows, entertaining your girl friend or boy friend, are all examples of not important but urgent activities.

These activities are not useful because it's not going to help you in achieving your goal. These are activities that a large percentage of average people spend their time on. But sometimes these activities also help relieve the everyday stress and relax.

Another phrase for this category is "distracters", because these are the activities that will interrupt you when you are doing other activities.

The way to avoid wasting your time this way is to go to a quiet place where you can have the minimum distractions such as switch off your hand phone or clear your table leaving only what you are going to do. That way you can minimize the number of distractions.

Not important and not urgent (IV)

There are also a lot of people who fall into this category. Activities like going to the arcade, playing computer games, watching movies, staring into the sky, all this are neither goal-directed nor urgent activities. Average people spend most of their time doing such activities and neglect the important things and thus there is always a gap between the successful people and average people.

Do successful people spend their time on these activities? Yes. But they spend most of their time on activities that are goal directed. It's only after they reach their goals that they take some time to enjoy themselves so they can work towards other goals.

So do you see the difference in taking time to enjoy and when you can do that? I always believe that you will need to work towards your goals while celebrating the small successes you achieve along the way. That way you can also enjoy while you continue working towards achieving your goals.

The key to prioritizing your time here is by spending your time mostly on (II) - Activities that are goal directed and not urgent. Successful people spend their time mostly on these.

How do we manage our time?

We would first require these 3 items.

1. a term calendar
2. weekly planner
3. Daily - to do list

When you first plan your time, start by listing the goals. And followed by listing what you would require to reach your goals. And then write down the number of topics that you are required to learn.

LIST DOWN YOUR GOALS

For example, I have listed down my goals and here are the following things that I would need to do before I can reach my goals.

1. Grade 8 piano 2007 – 1 hr/ day
2. To get As' for all the subjects – 100 topics
3. Fitness and health - Developing 6 packs abdomen
4. Social life – hang out with friends once a fortnight

Write down your topics

So for each of the topics, I roughly have an idea of how much time I need to spend on each activity. I shall go in detail with the study part first. Let us see how many topics we are going to cover.

Take this as an example
Mathematics E - 20
Mathematics A - 20
Chemistry - 20
Physics - 20
History - 10
Geography - 10

So in order to score well in my exams, the following activities are required –

1. read and understand (power read)
2. mind map
3. commit into memory
4. practice (applying)
5. revision

I would need to master and learn all the topics at least 2 months before the exams. My exams start around October which gave me around 8 months to learn and study. Therefore every month, I would require mastering around 2 topics of each subject.

Daily Activities to include in the daily-to-do list

Here's a look at the small activities I gave myself to commit for each day when I was taking my 'A' level.

1. revision or recall of the previous lessons in between classes

2. use free periods to finish up all the tutorials that have NOT been taught

3. after reaching home and settling down, spend a 15 minutes - 30 minutes to recall what the teachers taught in the class

4. start doing the important and urgent as first priority

5. do mind map and arranging questions

6. practice questions

7. do tutorials that are going to be taught

8. read up on next day lessons before going to bed

9. do some personal work to relax

10. revision of last week's homework and lessons

You may think this is madness. However, if you start this habit in the start of the year, you would have plenty of time each day later on for you to have more time to play and have fun. Of course I did not do all this at one shot.

I created this list because it's a good system that enables me to learn effectively, to memorize better so I won't have to waste more time learning from scratch.

So what do you do with your monthly calendar?

First you insert all the important dates such as your exam dates, important functions and roughly the time you are going to study for exams.

Next is your weekly planner.

Here is an important piece of information. You need to plan the weekly planner before you start the week in specific terms. You will write in it, how you are going to plan your time to study, how many mind maps you are going to do, how many questions you are practicing, how much time you are allocating on your studies etc.

It should also contain your homework, projects to be handed in, tests, and many more. Things to take note for a weekly planner

1. you are to allocate the right amount of time for each activity
2. not too much and not too little
3. before the end of the day, do your best to finish each activity
4. as you finish each of them, put a Big tick.
5. if you really can't finish, reallocate the activity to another day

The truth is that teachers are way behind me in their topics while teaching that I never actually had any important and urgent work to do. And I was always way ahead that I didn't need to spend much time studying for exams.

That was what actually happened in my college year. And guess what I spent my time on........... I wasted it on my girlfriend. (Well, I shall not go about it here)

How should you plan for your revision?

Most students face the problem of having too much to study before the exams. Some even wait till the last minute and use the excuse that they will forget if they start too early. Others face the problem of having no time to practice, or do not understand the topics well.

The top students are the ones that know how to arrange their time for revision and plan it so well that they have time to finish everything a week or more before the exams start.

The secret to revision is to start planning from the back instead of the front. What I mean is you should work backwards from the date of exams to where you are now.

Before the exams, you should do at least 4 revisions of each topic in every subject. Each revision should include recalling of the mind map, practicing of the questions, and reviewing the questions that are wrong.

The 4th revision should be 2 weeks after the 3rd revisions while the 3rd revisions should be 1 week after the second one. The 2nd one is just a day after the first one.

Here's a little example...

Let's say you are taking the following subjects, Maths, chemistry, physics, geography, history, and biology.

And these are the number of chapters.

Mathematics - 12
Chemistry - 10
Physics - 13
History - 7
Geography - 10
Biology – 9

It's essential to take down your exam dates and put it into your calendar. Once you have written down all your dates, you will be able to plan how much you are going to study each day.

Next, you will leave 7 days before all the examination free as emergency dates because just in case you have no time to finish, there's still 7 days more before your exams.

You can refer to the calendar below.

September 2006

SUN	MON	TUE	WED	THU	FRI	SAT
					1 Math 1 Math 2 Physics 1	2 math 3 Physics 2 Physics 3
3 Chem 1 Geog 1 History 1	4 Geog 2 Physics 4 Chemistry 2	5 History 2 Geog 2 Chem 3	6 Geog 3 Physics 5 Chemistry 4	7 Maths 4 History 3 Biology 5	8 Geog 5 Physics 6 Chemistry 5	9 Revision date 1-8
10 Maths 5 History 4 Biology 6	11 Geog 6 Physics 7 Chemistry 6	12 Maths 6 History 5 Biology 7	13 Geog 7 Physics 8 Chemistry 7	14 Geog 8 Physics 9 Chemistry 8	15 Maths 7 History 6 Biology 8	16 Revision (date 10-15)
17 Maths 8 History 7 Biology 9	18 Geog 9 Physics 10 Chemistry 9	19 Maths 9 maths 10	20 Geog 10 Physics 11 Chemistry 10	21 Physics 12	22 Revision (date 17-21)	23 Revision (date 1-8)
24 Revision (date 10-15)	25 Revision (date 17-21)	26	27	28	29	30

$\Leftarrow$ ――――― *emergency* ―――――

October 2006

SUN	MON	TUE	WED	THU	FRI	SAT
1 *emergency*	2	3	4	5 Geography Exam	6	7
8	9 Maths Exam	10 Biology Exam	11 Chemistry Exam	12	13 Physics Exam	14
15	16 History Exam	17	18	19	20	21
22	23	24	25	26	27	28
29	30	31				

Next, some students find it difficult to keep their level of concentration high. Some people like to call it attention deficit. Let me show you the way to keep your concentration level high.

CHAPTER 10

CONCENTRATION AND FOCUS: THE 'STEPPING STONES' TO SCORING A'S FASTER!

Congratulations for making it this far. You have proved that you have the desire to succeed. And most importantly, you have the discipline to read up to this chapter. This shows that you are determined to succeed. Keep it up!

From this chapter onwards, I am going to share with you strategies that will improve your concentration and focus when you are studying!

And for your information, these simple strategies have worked effectively for students who have suffered from Attention Disability Disorder Syndrome and hyperactivity. There is a lot of controversy surrounding these 2 issues which I don't wish to go into as it is beyond the scope of this book.

But my point here is that 'ADDS and hyperactivity' are merely labels (which destroys your real self-image). So drop them and start learning the **strategies to 'shape you' into staying concentrated and focused when studying.**

What affects your ability to concentrate and stay focused?

YOU (internal environment)

+

External Environment (surroundings)

= KEY to *Concentration and Focus*

This is the timeless formula that eludes many students. It's simple, humble but extremely effective! Let's begin exploring the 2 areas!

External Factor:
Setting up the *Optimal Study Environment*

The first habit to high concentration and focus is to have an optimal study environment where you find it comfortable to work. For those of you who do not have a place to go to for studying, start setting up one now.

Nothing fancy, but to start, you just need a desk and chair and away from any noise.

Some of you may be thinking about having your favorite chair, mug and stationery and that's really a small part of the equation. Those are just small accessories that add to your comfort.

Here are some characteristics you should have in your learning environment.

Brighten up with some good lighting

I am sure you know this was coming. Good lighting is important in a study environment. Poor lighting makes it strenuous for the eyes and it gets people sleepy after some time.

The ideal lighting would be natural sunlight that's neither too bright nor scorching hot. Hence, the next best choice of lighting is to have a mixture of white and yellow light. This should keep you awake and avoid any possible headaches since fluorescent (white) light is glaring and may cause headaches.

Keep the temperature cool

The brain works best at 19°Celsius. Temperatures that are too hot will make you feel drowsy while temperatures that are around 20-25°Celsius puts a person to sleep easily.

19° Celsius is a good temperature. Not too hot and not too cold. No drowsiness and sleepiness.

Avoid heavy eating

Now, this is an interesting point to make note of. When exams are around the corner, due to the increasing stress and pressure, students react to eating with great extremes. One group will lose their appetite and start eating less while another will have an

INCREASE in appetite to cope with the pressure. Both are bad. Start taking less food is equivalent to weakening your immune system while heavy eating before studying or taking exams puts the brain to sleep.

For maximum focus and optimal thinking, avoid heavy eating. Here are some food items to take note of if you want to maximize effectiveness when studying.

Avoid turkey, sugar, food with white flour, excessive caffeine and alcohol. This may sound silly but some students perceive their ideal study environment to be a comfortable place to the extent of having a few cans of beer on the desk. Alcohol is a strictly No-No!

No Multi-tasking when studying but Baroque Music is Ok!

"You can do only one thing at a time. I simply tackle one problem and concentrate all efforts on what I am doing at the moment."

Dr. Maxwell Maltz

Now, multi-tasking is another issue that needs to be addressed. The fastest way to get a thing done is to really put all your efforts into doing that one thing at that moment. This is especially so when it comes to studying. No internet chatting, no phone calls, no fiddling with your mobile phones but concentrate on studying at that given specific time slot!

However, playing some background music is RECOMMENDED only if you play Bach. Why play baroque music? It puts your brain into alpha state (relaxed state), making it more receptive to absorbing new knowledge.

Some examples of baroque music would be Antonio Vivaldi's Four Seasons, J.S. Bach's Fugue and many more. A quick way to listen to such baroque music is to get ** "Alpha- State Music" CDs.

Say NO to distractions

Your ideal study environment should be free from distractions. And that means no TV, magazines, video games, comics and hand phones. Make it a point to switch off your mobile phones every time you sit down to study.

The next BIGGEST distraction is the BED. Study in an environment where there is no bed for you to relax and lie on. Studying on the bed gets you too comfortable and relaxed for you to concentrate and focus for a long time.

Individual or group study

Another question most students have is to study alone or as a group? There is no right or wrong. It depends on you as well as the group. For maximum concentration and effectiveness, studying alone ensures minimal distraction.

Whereas studying in a group would definitely result in some distractions, this also facilitates the studying process through the exchange of notes and ideas with other students.

If you decide to study in a group, your goal must be to 'fly with the eagles'. Study with students that are focused in getting the 'studying' done and not those that get together in the name of studying but spend most of their time talking.

Morning or Night Study

Which time of the day gives me the best focus? This is really up to personal preference and study habits. Some students are 'morning' people, i.e. they are the most active and receptive to new knowledge in the morning and slightly sluggish in the night.

If you were to base on such a habit/trend, studying in the morning is the best for you. However, there is a point which I would like to highlight. Would you be choosing when to study if your exams are approaching?

Definitely NO! Most students would be studying throughout the day, day is night and night is day. In a nutshell, your internal environment is playing tricks on you. Anytime is a good time for maximum focus if you alter your internal environment, as long as the external environment is free from distractions. You just need to learn how to summon your best emotional state of mind when required.

And this brings us to the next factor... **Internal Environment!**

Internal Environment:
The *Central Command Center* for Concentration and Focus

The internal environment is about you.

In this section, we are going to explore how you can remain focused when studying ANYTIME.

Here are 2 scenarios for you to consider.

Scenario 1: Studying under pressure and stress

Scenario 2: Studying in a relaxed and confident manner

Which would you prefer? Which would result in higher level of concentration and focus? The answer should be obviously scenario 2!

Hence the first thing you have to pay attention to when you are about to study is your emotional state. For the best performance, strive to study in a relaxed and confident manner which empowers you with higher levels of concentration, focus and assimilation of information.

Here are several ways to take charge of your emotional state:

1. Controlling your internal dialogue.

Some students approach studies, with a string of negative thoughts in their mind. "Oh! I hate this subject!" "This is difficult. I get confused all the time!" And the result! You have already lost half the battle even before it could start!

Here is what I need you to do:
You have to start building your vocabulary for success by simply re-looking and reframing some of the negativity.

Negative: "This is difficult! I get confused every time!"
Positive: "This is challenging! Confuse is good, I am building new neuro-connections that will make me SMARTER!"

Negative: "Oh! I hate this subject!"
Positive: "No! I don't hate this subject! I just lack understanding over this subject!" or issue a challenge to yourself by saying "I am going to make this my best subject!"

These are just some examples. By taking charge of your internal dialogue, you will have power over your emotional state. Would you not be then more optimistic, relaxed and confident? Try this the next time you are about to study a new subject or one that you don't like but have to study. Put yourself in an optimistic state before beginning.

2. Behave like an 'A' student!

The next strategy is about taking charge of your actions.

How do you sit and walk when you are in a lousy mood? Slow... tired... slouching... with absolutely no energy. Observe the actions, posture and behavior of an 'A' student and compare it with an average student in class.

There should be a significant difference. If possible, observe them when they are studying independently for exams. Posture would be upright, eyes beaming with confidence and energy level high.

Your actions account to your emotional state. Hence, make sure you behave confidently the next time you are about to study by having some good body posture at least to give this technique a good start.

3. Focus

What you focus on affects your emotional state. 'A' students visualize an enjoyable study process and a successful outcome. This puts them in a relaxed and confident state.

'B', 'C', 'D' students visualize 'impending doom' or a frustrating experience at the start of the study session. Stress, pressure and tensions build up quickly. You have short- circuited yourself greatly because of your mental make up.

Try this in the next study session

Close your eyes before you begin. Visualize the outcome of your session. What would you say at the end? How would you stretch your body? What would you look at?

Then work backwards. What would be the study process/session like? Visualize your posture, breathing and energy.

This may sound 'irrelevant' to you but it works if you are not trained to approach studying in an optimistic and confident mode every time! Take about 5 minutes to complete this exercise. It will be of great help.

Do all these exercises each time you begin studying. They will empower your study in its peak state.

Pacing Yourself to Stay Focused

Some students study non-stop for 2 hours only to find that 50% of their time is productive. And the remaining 1 hour is spent fighting distraction or probably finding themselves daydreaming.

Research has shown that an ideal study session should be no longer than 2 hours. And this study session should be further broken down into four, 20-30 minute periods. After every period, take a mini break of about 2 to 5 minutes.

By pacing yourself by taking mini breaks at every 20-30 minutes interval, you will boost your concentration and the ability to recall what you have studied. And this will result in a more effective use of your study time.

During the study breaks, it is strongly recommend that you do some relaxation exercises. Simple exercises are highly recommended. Get off your seat, move your body a little, get the blood flowing or go grab a nutritious drink for uplifting your mood.

After each 2 hour session, relax for half an hour.

By sticking to such a study session, you will enjoy a more pleasurable study experience as you would have the luxury to take mini breaks to refresh yourself. This will give you greater focus and ability to recall, allowing you to fully absorb what you have learnt effectively.

There you have it. I have told you all. Master them and you can expect to have control over your emotional state.

CONCLUSION:

PUTTING UP YOUR 'STUDY BATTLE PLAN'

Congratulations. You have made it to the final step. There is one invisible barrier left to overcome and that is to take action.

Now, there are 3 possible scenarios likely to happen for any student who has read this book.

1. You don't feel motivated enough to take action. So you procrastinate. And you decide to leave this book in your hard disk to collect digital dust. You are aware of the learning strategies but you simply don't make the effort to implement them in your life. That's really fine with me since you are the one taking the exams.

2. The motivated ones will take action... but they do it in a disorganized way. They jump into the bandwagon without knowing where it is heading. There is no consistency in their learning. Picking up bits and pieces along the way and applying them would be characteristics of their approach. My guess is that they will see some results, but because they lack mastery over the skills, getting 'As' is still a challenge.

3. You are motivated, you are all 'pumped up' and ready for action. Bravo! (I am happy for you!) And you understand the fact that 'A' students take time to plan their course of action. You carefully mapped out what needs to be picked up and apply over a period of 1-3 months, depending on the time you set aside as well as your level of desire.

If you are in scenario 3, you are ready for the next section...

Mapping out your 'Study Battle Plan'

Here is a re-cap in general.

1. Goal Setting

2. Learning Strategies

3. Time management strategies

This is a simplified version of the structure and contents found in this book. And if you have done the exercises instructed earlier on, you must have a mini plan in your hands now. Some fine-tuning and you are ready to go!

Final Goal Setting Strategies In A nutshell

A goal without a plan is just a wish.
Antoine de Saint-Exupery

To guide you along, here are some questions for you to think and answer. The questions are the answers. Hence think both long term and short term.

1. What do you want to achieve from your studies? What is your expectation level? What is your satisfactory level? What do you want to score for your next test/exam?

2. Why do you want to do all the above? Find convincing and compelling reasons. Don't sugarcoat your reasons. Personal reasons are more compelling. For example, "I want to score 'As' because I don't want to be looked down upon by my friends." The feelings of embarrassment and humiliation are definitely better triggers for motivation.

3. When do you want to reach those goals? Set a reasonable deadline. You can't score As' overnight. You can't learn all the learning strategies overnight.

4. Who would be good roles models to follow? This book is about accelerating your way to success in studies. Finding role models to observe and follow is a good strategy as well. Observe his mind set, beliefs, how he behaves when he is learning new materials and integrate them into the knowledge you have learnt from this book. You can do this for sports as well.

5. Where can you find these role models? There will definitely be one or two in class. Where else do they hang out? Library! Then talk to them. Find out more about their study habits. What about those who seem to get 'As' without trying? Go find and talk to them. Ask the appropriate questions.

6. How are you going to execute the strategies found in this book? Just dive in head first and see what happens?

That will lead to bad execution. You need to set aside a certain amount of time everyday to put the strategies into use! But how much time do you need to set aside?

It really depends on your level of desire! Here are a few guidelines.

1. Start applying the strategies by order, i.e. to start with power reading followed by mind mapping.

2. Set aside a minimum of 30 minutes a day to focus on developing one learning strategy. Motivated students do as much as 2 hours a day for each strategy.

3. After a week's training, you should see some improvement.

4. Apply the Ultimate Success Formula as you try finding ways to improve your learning process.

5. Move on to the next learning strategy. Some strategies would come more naturally while one or two may take a longer time to master.

6. The key is to be consistent in your learning and application of these strategies.

7. Don't give up mid-way. When you find it tough and are losing motivation, search for compelling reasons to carry on.

8. Do this for a month and you would have reached a level of competence allowing you to apply them in your studies and have *immediate* results.

The above is a general guideline you can start working on. Start setting up a plan for your course of action. **Improve on the plan as you go... Build momentum in carrying out your plans.**

This book can only bring you to this point. Your journey of this book has ended. Now bring these strategies into school and create your outcomes and benefits from what you want from your studies.

We wish you the very best of luck!

Made in the USA
Las Vegas, NV
08 October 2021